Jonathan M. Klick

University of Maryland at College Park

Revised and Updated by Joan M. McElroy

STUDY GUIDE AND MAP WORKBOOK

D1567290

Out of Many

FOURTH EDITION

A History of the American People

Volume II

John Mack Faragher
Yale University

Mari Jo Buhle
Brown University

Daniel Czitrom
Mount Holyoke College

Susan H. Armitage
Washington State University

PRENTICE HALL, *Upper Saddle River, NJ 07458*

© 2003 by PEARSON EDUCATION, INC.
Upper Saddle River, New Jersey 07458

10 9 8 7 6 5 4 3 2 1

ISBN 0-13-098927-4
Printed in the United States of America

TABLE OF CONTENTS

PREFACE TO THE STUDENT: STUDY FORMAT

This study guide is meant to complement, not replace, the textbook *Out of Many: A History of the American People,* fourth edition by John Mack Faragher, Mari Jo Buhle, Daniel Czitrom, and Susan H. Armitage. If used effectively, the study guide can help your study of American history proceed more smoothly and efficiently.

Before you begin reading each chapter, it would be profitable to review the relevant **Survey/Chapter Overview** in this study guide and the **Chapter Outline** and **Key Topics** at the beginning of each chapter in the textbook. These sections will serve as your map to the text, which, due to the wealth of information it contains, can often become overwhelming. By knowing where you are headed before hand, your journey through the text will be greatly simplified.

You'll notice that each chapter of the study guide also suggests that you use the **Chronology** at the end of each chapter in the textbook as a way to get oriented before you start reading the chapter. Chapter 17 of the study guide provides a list of standard questions to ask as you review the Chronology. Questions concerning the chronology of events are of great importance because dates and relative orderings of events create the context of history.

The **Questions/Read** section of the guide is organized around the major subheadings of the chapter outline. Under each subheading are three ways to help you stay focused on the most important information in each section as you read the chapter. The first is a list of a few key questions about the main ideas that is written in the form of objectives or tasks that you should be able to accomplish after you have read the text and done the appropriate **Study Skills** exercises. These questions are followed by a list of key terms and people to identify. These identifications provide the details that support the main ideas covered in the questions. There are tips in the **Study Skills** section of Chapter 18 of the study guide to help you make the most of identifications. Finally, there are Map Exercises to do because maps appear in each section of the textbook. The map exercises can be particularly profitable because often geography is the major force that drives the development of history. If you read over the appropriate section of the study guide before you begin reading the textbook, you'll know what to look for as you read.

The **Study Skills Exercises** section provides a back-end check on your retention and understanding of the material in the chapter. There are practical tips to help you improve your study habits as well as questions that help you deepen your understanding of the textbook material. A careful analysis of the text should enable you to answer all of the questions in this section. You may find areas of weakness that could be remedied before you take any formal examinations on the material. This section includes both objective and subjective questions and extended essay topics.

In summary, the following is the standard outline for all Study Guide chapters.

SURVEY
>	Chapter Overview
>	Chronology

QUESTIONS/READ
>	Main Headings of the Textbook
>	Identifications
>	Map Exercises

STUDY SKILLS EXERCISES

The following will be included in each chapter. (There may be additional exercises called Study Tips in the earlier chapters.)

Vocabulary

Making Connections

Reflections

RECITE/REVIEW

Multiple Choice, including Map and Chronology Questions

Short Essay

Extended Essay

Answers to Multiple Choice (with text page numbers) and text page number references for Essay Questions

PREFACE TO *OUT OF MANY*

The text's authors use the theme of community throughout this textbook. It will be helpful for you to read the Preface and other introductory material on pages xxi–xxii and the essay "Community and Diversity" starting on page xxviii of the textbook to understand the authors' approach and to help you answer the following questions.

1. How can American history be viewed as a struggle for community?

2. What is the definition of community?

3. How has community been reinvented rather than lost?

4. What is the underlying dialectic of this textbook?

5. What is acculturation and what has encouraged it?

6. How do barbecues illustrate acculturation?

7. What are the ideas of John Dewey and Horace Kallen on American history and diversity?

8. What is the basic plan of this textbook?

9. What special features are offered in this textbook?

10. How is this textbook different from other American history texts?

17 Reconstruction, 1863–1877

SURVEY

Chapter Overview: If you skipped the first section of this study guide, please read the Preface to the Student before starting this section. This study guide is based on a particular study method and you will get more out of it if you read the explanatory material as well as the Preface to your textbook.

Reconstruction was a conflict in three areas. The first area was who was to conduct it—the executive or the legislative branch. This led to political battles between Johnson and the Radical Republicans. The second area was between Radical Republicans and a white South that refused to be reconstructed. The third area of conflict was between blacks and whites, with the latter trying to diminish any gains of the former slaves by enacting black codes and by condoning groups such as the Ku Klux Klan. Eventually, Reconstruction would fail because the Radicals lost the will to struggle and the Republican Party became more identified with business. A disputed election in 1877 ended in a compromise that allowed Hayes to take the presidency if federal troops were withdrawn from the South.

Before you begin reading, turn to the CHRONOLOGY at the end of the chapter. Don't try to memorize it. Use the following questions to orient yourself in space and time and understand who the leading characters are in the story this chapter will tell. Look for cause and effect relationships. Note unfamiliar terms that you will be learning about. You may want to bookmark this page so you can refer to it as you study the chapter. When you have finished reading this chapter, come back to these questions and see how much better you understand them.

- What time span is being covered and what is its significance?
- What are the major events covered in this chapter and how do they relate to one another? How do they connect to the chapter title?
- Who are the significant people as groups or as individuals involved in these events?
- What are the significant places?
- What important terms and concepts are connected to these events?

You will be referred back to these questions in each future chapter of this study guide.

QUESTIONS/READ

As you read each section, use the questions to help you focus on the major themes. Use them as a way to organize note-taking as you read. The objective is for you to be able to answer these questions after you have read the chapter and completed the study skills exercises. Be on the lookout for important terms that you should be able to identify (see the study skills section in Chapter 18 of the Study Guide for tips on how to fully identify these important terms), and do the map exercises as you go along.

AMERICAN COMMUNITIES:

- Describe the problems of community in Hale Country, Alabama as typical of the struggle in the South after the Civil War.
- **Identify:** Union League, Ku Klux Klan, "Second Reconstruction"

THE POLITICS OF RECONSTRUCTION:

- Compare the Reconstruction plans of Lincoln and Johnson to the plan of the Radical Republicans and explain how the feuding led to impeachment of President Johnson.
- Outline the major political issues in Reconstruction. What was and was not solved by the Civil War?
- Describe the state of the South after the war.
- Explain how this era was a turning point for women's suffrage. How did the views of Susan B. Anthony and Elizabeth Cady Stanton compare to Lucy Stone and Frederick Douglass?
- **Identify:** Proclamation of Amnesty and Reconstruction, Ten Percent Plan, Wade-Davis bill, Butler's policy, Field Order 15, Freedmen's Bureau, Thirteenth Amendment, John Wilkes Booth, "Black Codes," George W. Julian, Thaddeus Stevens, Joint Committee on Reconstruction, Civil Rights Act and Freedmen's Bureau, Fourteenth Amendment, "waving the bloody shirt," Fifteenth Amendment, Equal Rights Association, American Woman Suffrage Association, National Woman Suffrage Association
- **Map exercise:** *Reconstruction of the South, 1866–1877:* (p. 505) What types of districts were established in 1867 in the South? What southern state was first to be readmitted and also have the Democrats returned to power?

THE MEANING OF FREEDOM:

- Discuss the issues of freedom for African Americans after the Civil War.
- Describe the role of family, church, school, and politics in the lives of African Americans after the Civil War.
- Describe the type of laboring and farming system that replaced the old plantation system.
- **Identify:** "wayside schools," AMA, Tougaloo-Hampton-Fisk, "forty acres and a mule," North Carolina Freedmen's Convention, First Reconstruction Act, Union League
- **Map exercise:** *The Barrow Plantation, Oglethorpe County, Georgia, 1860 and 1881:* (p. 513) What changes are evident from 1860 to 1881 due to emancipation?

SOUTHERN POLITICS AND SOCIETY:

- Summarize the problems in reconstructing the seceded states.
- Compare the Republicans goals for the South with what actually occurred.
- Explain how Democrats regained control of southern politics by 1877.
- Describe how the southern social system worked to reinforce dependence on cotton and the crop lien system.
- **Identify:** carpetbaggers, scalawags, "confiscation radicals," the "gospel of prosperity," Ku Klux Klan Act, "redeemed States," Slaughterhouse Cases, *U.S. v. Reese, U.S. v. Cruikshank,* Civil Rights Cases
- **Map exercise:** *Southern Sharecropping, 1880:* (p. 519) Which areas and states had the most sharecropping arrangements?

RECONSTRUCTING THE NORTH:

- Trace the changes in the North and in the federal government away from Reconstruction, and include the Electoral Crisis of 1876 and the Compromise of 1877.
- Describe the place of the railroads in the Age of Capital and what effects railroad construction had on the North and South. How was the railroad industry related to the Depression of 1873?
- **Identify:** Promontory Point, Pennsylvania Railroad, Cornelius Vanderbilt, Crédit Mobilier, National Mineral Act of 1866, Standard Oil, Tweed Ring, Liberal Republicans, Charles Francis Adams, "Root, Hog, or Die," Horace Greeley, "tramp," Chicago's Citizens' Association, "Compromise of 1877," Samuel J. Tilden, Rutherford B. Hayes, "Whiskey Ring," "home rule"
- **Map exercise:** *The Election of 1876:* (p. 524) Which states had disputed votes?

CONCLUSION:

- Evaluate the successes and failures of Reconstruction.

REVIEW QUESTIONS: Use these and the chapter objectives to check your grasp of the major chapter themes. It is good practice to write out essay answers to these questions.

STUDY SKILLS EXERCISES

1. Vocabulary:

antebellum, p. 500	integrated, p. 516
centralization, p. 505	incendiary, p. 517
obstructionism, p. 506	panic, p. 523
denominations, p. 511	

2. Making Connections:

- To what extent did both the North and the South continue the economic divisions and sectionalism of the antebellum period in the postwar period?
- Discuss the problems of restructuring the southern society after the Civil War and the ending of slavery in light of the historic development of the South. (Chapters Four, Eleven, Fifteen)

3. Reflection: Imagine yourself as a teacher in the Freedmen's Bureau. What would you have thought you could contribute to Reconstruction?

RECITE/REVIEW

REVIEW QUESTIONS: This section has a sampling of multiple choice, short essay, and extended essay questions that you should be able to answer when you have completed the chapter and used other study techniques. To help you in reviewing the material, questions have been grouped according to the major sections of the chapter. Of course, you cannot expect your tests to be set up in this way.

▶ AMERICAN COMMUNITIES ◀

Multiple Choice

1. The freed African Americans represented what fraction of the total southern population?
    a. one tenth
    b. one fourth
    c. one third
    d. one half

▶ THE POLITICS OF RECONSTRUCTION ◀

Multiple Choice

2. Lincoln's Proclamation of Amnesty and Reconstruction was called the Ten Percent Plan. This number referred to the percentage of
    a. southerners swearing loyalty to the Constitution.
    b. blacks who would be allowed to vote.
    c. lands redistributed to blacks on a homestead basis.
    d. Republican Party members in each reconstructed state.

3. Both Lincoln and Johnson shared the view that Reconstruction
    a. should punish the South for secession.
    b. was a presidential function.
    c. needed to be a complete socio-economic transformation.
    d. prohibited any real conciliation of North and South.

4. Which one of the following is the RESULT of the other three?
    a. President Johnson impeached
    b. Tenure of Office Act passed
    c. Civil Rights Act passed
    d. Reconstruction Acts passed

5. Which two states met Lincoln's requirements for readmission to the Union before the end of the war but were denied by Congress?
    a. Virginia and Maryland
    b. North and South Carolina
    c. Kentucky and Tennessee
    d. Arkansas and Louisiana

6. The Fourteenth Amendment was passed to ensure the constitutionality of
    a. the Wade-Davis bill.
    b. the Freedmen's Bureau.
    c. the Civil Rights Act of 1866.
    d. the First Reconstruction Act.

7. Which one of the following states had NOT been readmitted to the Union by 1868?
    a. Florida
    b. North Carolina
    c. Virginia
    d. South Carolina

8. Which one of the following statements is true?
    a. The African American vote played no role in the election of 1868.
    b. The Democrats opposed Reconstruction.
    c. Violence was used to prevent southern Democrats from voting.
    d. Grant won 75 percent of the popular vote in 1868.

Map Question
9. The first southern state to be readmitted with the Democrats in power was
    a. Tennessee.
    b. Florida.
    c. Texas.
    d. Georgia.

Short Essay
10. How did the Union try to redistribute southern land to African Americans?

11. Why did many politicians oppose universal suffrage?

Extended Essay
12. Discuss the factors leading to President Johnson's impeachment.

13. Describe how the battle over the Fourteenth and Fifteenth Amendments affected the women's suffrage movement.

Multiple Choice

14. By 1880, nearly three quarters of black southerners became
    a. Democrats.
    b. factory workers.
    c. "redeemers."
    d. sharecroppers.

15. Between 1865 and 1870, the African American population in the South's ten largest cities
    a. doubled.
    b. was cut in half.
    c. stayed the same.
    d. grew by 25 percent.

16. The greatest change in gender roles of African American families during Reconstruction was
    a. greater equality between husband and wife.
    b. more women working in the fields.
    c. assertion of authority by African American men.
    d. more single-parent families headed by women.

17. The first social institution fully controlled by African Americans was
    a. the school.
    b. the church.
    c. the Freedmen's Bureau.
    d. the southern Republican Party.

18. The literacy rate among African Americans in 1860 was
    a. over 90 percent.
    b. less than 10 percent.
    c. 25 percent.
    d. 75 percent.

Map Question

19. Which one of the following statements is true about the Barrow Plantation in Oglethorpe County Georgia?
    a. In 1881, no members of the Barrow family were still living on the Barrow Plantation.
    b. In 1860, slave families lived in individual houses spread all over the plantation.
    c. In 1881, former slaves had their own church and school on the plantation.
    d. The layout of houses in 1881 shows the extended family had little importance in the African American community.

Short Essay

20. Compare the wage sharing and sharecropping systems of labor that was preferred by African Americans.

21. Describe African American politics during Reconstruction.

Extended Essay

22. Discuss the meaning of freedom for African Americans of this period. Was the freedom a real freedom, or was it freedom in name only?

▶SOUTHERN POLITICS AND SOCIETY◀

Multiple Choice

23. Which one of the following is NOT one of the three groups that made up the fledgling Republican coalition in the postwar South?
    a. African Americans
    b. Radical Democrats
    c. white northerners
    d. prewar Whigs

24. If you lived in eastern Tennessee, western North Carolina, or northern Alabama and were a small farmer, you were most likely to be in a group derisively called
    a. tramps.
    b. redemptioners.
    c. carpetbaggers.
    d. scalawags.

25. In the southern state constitutional conventions called under the First Reconstruction Act, the largest majority of delegates were
    a. southern white Republicans.
    b. northern white Republicans.
    c. newly freed African Americans.
    d. antebellum free African Americans.

26. Which one of the following Supreme Court cases is not correctly paired with the amendment or law that it limited?
    a. Slaughterhouse Cases/Fourteenth Amendment
    b. U.S. vs. Reese/Ku Klux Klan Act
    c. U.S. vs. Cruikshank/Fifteenth Amendment
    d. Civil Rights Cases/Thirteenth Amendment

27. Which one of the following statements is true?
    a. Pent-up demand increased the prices for cotton immediately after the Civil War.
    b. Cotton prices rose with the expansion of the cotton crop after the Civil War.
    c. After the Civil War, southern cotton was still the leader on the international market.
    d. Per capita wealth in the South was equal to other farming regions of the country.

Map Question

28. Which one of the following was NOT a state in which sharecropping became most pervasive?
    a. Georgia
    b. Alabama
    c. Texas
    d. North Carolina

Short Essay

29. Explain the connection between African Americans' hope for land and railroads in the Reconstruction South.

30. How did the federal government deal with the Ku Klux Klan between 1870 and 1872?

Extended Essay

31. Describe the role of King Cotton in the South after the Civil War.

▶ RECONSTRUCTING THE NORTH ◀

Multiple Choice

32. In 1877, the same year that federal troops were withdrawn from the South, they were used in the North to
    a. repress Ku Klux Klan sympathizers.
    b. restore control after a race riot in New York City.
    c. break a violent national railroad strike.
    d. drive any remaining eastern Indians to western reservations.

33. The first big businesses in America were the
    a. mining companies.
    b. oil companies.
    c. railroad companies.
    d. steel mills.

34. Which one of the following has the LEAST in common with the other three?
    a. Crédit Mobilier
    b. Tweed Ring
    c. Whiskey Ring
    d. Confiscation Radicals

35. The Chicago's Citizens' Association had the MOST in common with
    a. E. L. Godkin and Horace Greeley.
    b. Andrew Johnson and Edwin Stanton.
    c. New York labor leaders and workers.
    d. Orville Babcock and William W. Belknap.

36. Which one of the following is the RESULT of the other three?
    a. Electoral Commission elects Hayes president
    b. election between Tilden and Hayes disputed
    c. federal troops withdrawn from the South
    d. Compromise of 1877

37. Which one of the following was NOT one of the Liberal Republicans' values?
    a. free trade
    b. defense of property rights
    c. continued federal intervention in the South
    d. civil service reform

38. Which one of the following was NOT a result of the Compromise of 1877?
    a. Hayes became president
    b. additional support for the Fourteenth and Fifteenth Amendments
    c. more money for southern internal improvements
    d. support of "home rule" in the South

Map Question
39. Which one of the following states did NOT have disputed electoral votes in the election of 1876?
    a. Oregon
    b. Florida
    c. California
    d. South Carolina

Short Essay
40. What role did the railroads play in the settlement of the West?

41. In what ways does Boss Tweed represent urban politics during this period?

Extended Essay

42. Why did black leaders not fight for integrated public schools during this period?

▶ CHRONOLOGY QUESTIONS ◀

Multiple Choice

43. Which one of the following events is NOT correctly matched to the year in which it took place?
    a. Thirteenth Amendment ratified/1865
    b. Ku Klux Klan Act passed/1868
    c. Fifteenth Amendment ratified/1870
    d. Slaughterhouse Cases/1873

44. The Union and Central Pacific meet at Promontory Point in Utah Territory in
    a. 1866.   c. 1872.
    b. 1869.   d. 1877.

45. Which one of the following lists the correct chronological order of events?
    (1) Democrats win control of House of Representatives
    (2) Ku Klux Klan founded
    (3) split in women's suffrage movement
    (4) Liberal Republicans nominate Horace Greeley

    a. 3, 1, 4, 2   c. 3, 2, 1, 4
    b. 2, 3, 4, 1   d. 2, 1, 3, 4

46. Congressional Reconstruction lasted for
    a. two years.
    b. five years.
    c. ten years.
    d. 12 years.

ANSWERS—CHAPTER 17

American Communities
    1. c, p. 498

The Politics of Reconstruction
    2. a, p. 501
    3. b, pp. 502–503
    4. a, pp. 505–506
    5. d, p. 501
    6. c, pp. 504–505
    7. c, p. 506
    8. b, pp. 506–507
    9. a, p. 505
    10. pp. 501–502
    11. pp. 501, 506–507
    12. pp. 505–507
    13. pp. 507–508

The Meaning of Freedom
    14. d, p. 512
    15. a, p. 509
    16. c, p. 510
    17. b, p. 511
    18. b, p. 511
    19. c, p. 513
    20. p. 512
    21. pp. 512–514
    22. pp. 509–514

Southern Politics and Society
    23. b, p. 515
    24. d, p. 515
    25. a, p. 515
    26. d, p. 518
    27. a, p. 520
    28. d, p. 519
    29. p. 516
    30. p. 518
    31. pp. 518–520

Reconstructing the North
    32. c, p. 521
    33. c, p. 522
    34. d, pp. 504, 522–524
    35. a, p. 524
    36. c, p. 524–525
    37. c, pp. 522–523
    38. b, p. 526
    39. c, p. 524

    40. pp. 521–522
    41. p. 522
    42. p. 516

Chronology Questions
    43. b, p. 525
    44. b, p. 525
    45. b, p. 525
    46. c, p. 525

18 Conquest and Survival: The Trans-Mississippi West, 1860–1900

SURVEY

Chapter Overview: This chapter covers the changes in transportation and technology that enabled white settlers to move into the trans-Mississippi West, an area viewed earlier as the Great American Desert and occupied by Indians and Mexicans. Mining, commercial farming, and ranching brought in more settlers as homestead laws and railroad land advertising promoted the settlement of the Great Plains. Indian communities were under siege and the Indians generally were pushed onto reservations. As the primitive West disappeared, parts of it were preserved in national parks, paintings, written works, photography, and a stereotyped Wild West. Indian cultures were seriously affected by the Dawes Act, but they managed to endure and rejuvenate.

Before you begin reading, turn to the CHRONOLOGY at the end of the chapter. Review it to orient yourself in space and time and understand who the leading characters are in the story this chapter will tell. Look for cause and effect relationships. Note unfamiliar terms that you will be learning about. Use the tips and questions at the beginning of Chapter 17 of the Study Guide as a guide for your use of the time line. Return to the CHRONOLOGY after you have read the chapter to see how much you have learned.

QUESTIONS/READ

As you read each section, use the questions to help you focus on the major themes. Use them as a way to organize note-taking as you read. The objective is for you to be able to answer these questions after you have read the chapter and completed the study skills exercises. Be on the lookout for important terms that you should be able to identify (see the study skills section in this chapter of the Study Guide for tips on how to fully identify these important terms), and do the map exercises as you go along.

AMERICAN COMMUNITIES:
- Explain how the Oklahoma Land Rush illustrated the effects of increased settlement on old and new communities in the trans-Mississippi West.
- **Identify:** Five Civilized Tribes, No Man's Land, "Boomers," "Soddies," Curtis Act
- **Map exercise:** *Oklahoma Territory:* (p. 531) What variety of Indian tribes were in Oklahoma Territory? What areas were affected by the land runs?

INDIAN PEOPLES UNDER SEIGE:
- Outline the various Indian peoples that populated the West, including their locations and populations.
- Describe the impact on and transformation of the Indian communities in the trans-Mississippi West. Carry this theme throughout the chapter and connect it especially with the last section of the chapter.
- **Identify:** *Cherokee Nation* v. *Georgia,* Indian Territory, Isaac Stevens, Medicine Lodge Treaty

of 1867, Lakota, vision seekers, Black Kettle, Sand Creek Massacre, Bozeman Trail, Great Sioux War, Red Cloud, Treaty of Fort Laramie, W. T. Sherman, Crazy Horse, Sitting Bull, George Custer, Little Bighorn, Greasy Grass, *Paba Sapa,* Cochise, Geronimo, Red River War, Nez Percé, Chief Tukekas, Chief Joseph, Wallowa

- **Map exercise:** *Major Indian Battles and Indian Reservations, 1860–1900:* (p. 533) Locate the Indian Tribes and battles referred to in the text. What was the result for Indian and white populations?

THE INTERNAL EMPIRE:

- Discuss the West as an internal empire—including the role of the federal government in its acquisition.
- Describe mining as an industry and as a type of community, and show its effect on westward expansion and on the environment.
- Describe Mormon settlement patterns and how Mormons structured their community and their agriculture.
- Compare the old and new communities of the Southwest and indicate any tensions that developed.
- **Identify:** Comstock Lode, Anaconda Copper Mining Company, Virginia City, Butte, "Helldorados," Caminetti Act, Joseph Smith, Brigham Young, Deseret, Utah Territory, *United States* v. *Reynolds,* Edmunds Act, Edmunds-Tucker Act, Gadsden Purchase, Treaty of Guadalupe Hidalgo, Sante Fe Ring, Estevan Ochoa, Amadors, Juan Cortina, Cortina's War, Las Corras Blancas, *El Alianzo Hispano-Americano, Mutualistes, Cinco de Mayo*
- **Map exercises:** *Railroad Routes, Cattle Trails, Gold and Silver Rushes, 1860–1890:* (p. 538) What were the names of the major railroads and cattle trails that crossed the West? In what direction did the cattle drives move? Where were gold and silver mines located? *Mormon Cultural Diffusion:* (p. 540) What areas of the West were permeated by Mormon settlements?

THE CATTLE INDUSTRY:

- Explain why the cattle industry developed when it did and evaluate its success.
- Describe various members of the cattle industry community and explain the causes of violence and instability.
- **Identify:** Joseph McCoy, Jesse Chisholm, Wyatt Earp, range wars

FARMING COMMUNITIES ON THE PLAINS:

- Summarize the impact of settlement on existing communities as well as the creation of new ones.
- Evaluate the impact of the Homestead Act on various locations and groups.
- Describe the groups that settled the plains, how the railroad contributed to their settlement, and what their lives were like.
- **Identify:** Hutterites, Oddfellows-Elks-Templars, Eastern Star-Companions of the Forest, one room school
- **Map exercise:** *The Establishment of National Parks and Forests:* (p. 552) Compare the relative size of national parks and forests east and west of the Mississippi. What was the earliest national park? national forest?

THE WORLD'S BREADBASKET:

- Outline the agricultural changes from the Plains to cattle industry to California including effects on the Midwest and East. Look back at earlier sections to fully complete this task.
- Describe the effects of increased settlement on the land of the West.
- **Identify:** John Deere, Cyrus McCormick, Morrill Act of 1862, Department of Agriculture, Weather Bureau, Hatch Act of 1887, 98th meridian, Oliver Dalrymple, Sunkist, Paul Masson, Sun Maid, Timber Culture Act, National Reclamation Act, Lake Tulare, Forest Service, General Land Revision Act of 1891, Forest Management Act

THE WESTERN LANDSCAPE:

- Summarize the efforts to create images of the primitive West in writings, paintings, photography, natural parks, and in stereotyped images of the Wild West.
- Explain the significance of the western region and its people to Americans in general.
- **Identify:** William H. Jackson, Thomas Moran, Yellowstone, Alfred Bierstadt, Edward Zane Carroll Judson, dime novels, Nat Love, Deadwood Dick, Calamity Jane, Joseph McCoy, William F. Cody, Owen Wister's *The Virginian,* Charles Schreyvogel, Charles Russell, Frederic Remington, Edward Sheriff Curtis, Lewis Henry Morgan, Alice Cunningham Fletcher, Suzette La Flesche, Boy and Girl Scouts

THE TRANSFORMATION OF INDIAN SOCIETIES:

- Explain the causes and the nature of the transformation of various Indian societies.
- **Identify:** Helen Hunt Jackson, *A Century of Dishonor,* Dawes Severalty Act, Indian Rights Association, WNIA, the Ghost Dance, Wovoka, Wounded Knee Creek, Big Foot, Black Elk, Navajo, Hopi, Pimas, Yanas, Flatheads, Quapaws, Cheyennes, "Dine," "Long Walk," potlatch

CONCLUSION:

- Explain what the transformation of the trans-Mississippi West meant for America.

REVIEW QUESTIONS: Use these to check your grasp of the major chapter themes. It is good practice to write out essay answers to these questions.

CHRONOLOGY: What time span is being covered? What is the significance of this particular time span? What are the major events covered in this chapter? How do they connect to the chapter title? Who are the significant people as groups or as individuals involved in these events? What are the significant places? What important terms and concepts are connected to these events?

NOTE: Since these questions are always the same, they will not be repeated after this chapter. I will just remind you to use these standard questions.

STUDY SKILLS EXERCISES

1. Vocabulary:

assimilation, p. 532	intrinsic, p. 545
nomadic, p. 535	coffer, p. 547
sabotaged, p. 540	lampooned, p. 554
cohesion, p. 541	eradicate, p. 557
bonanza, p. 543	tenacious, p. 558

2. **Study Tip:** In the preface of this guide, the skill of identification was mentioned as a useful way to study history. Use the pattern of who or what, when, where, and why in identifying major items. You can put these terms on 3x5 cards or use the Cornell method. Be sure to incorporate any pertinent material from illustrations or maps. It may also be useful to blend in material from various parts of the chapter or chapters. Do not expect all relevant material to be in one place. Try this method with the Dawes Severalty Act on pages 557–559 and see how your answer compares to the item below. Note that I left out the "how", but if your professor has numerous essay questions, the "how" might be included.

> *Dawes Severalty Act*
> **Who** or **What:** a law passed by Congress
> **When:** 1887—policy until 1934
> **Where:** to cover Indians on reservation lands
> **Why:** to break up tribes by giving land to individual Indians in order to force them to assimilate to white culture and become citizens. Reformers mistakenly hoped it would help, but it undermined tribal culture and resulted in a 60 percent loss of reservation lands and a 66 percent loss of individual allotments.

If your professor asks you to write short identification answers on a test, you should take the above information and blend it into a smooth paragraph as you write it out.

3. Remember to pay attention to **maps, graphs, and illustrations.** They can give you context and cues to understand and remember the material. For example, in this chapter, when you read about increased productivity of the farmer, you should also look at the chart on page 549 labeled "Hand v. Machine Labor on the Farm." What conclusions can you draw from it in relation to the text?

   Maps: If you are not quickly familiar with the locations of the western states, use one of the blank maps at the back of this study guide to practice naming them. The text authors assume you are geographically literate. If your professor has map tests, there are a variety of blank practice maps for you to photocopy at the end of the study guide.

4. **Making Connections:** In the preface, I mentioned reducing and rearranging information. One way to do this is to make a chart. A chart helps you compare and connect information. There are major advantages to doing this. First, you have elements of the entire chapter in a compact form to which you can add relevant lecture information. The second advantage is that doing a chart reinforces the material either for objective or essay exams. The third advantage is that you are actively involved in the material as you construct your charts. You can see the connections between things. I have put an example of a chart for you at the end of this chapter. Be alert to others that you can develop. You should have brief phrases or terms that remind you of the subject. Remember that your goal is summary. DO NOT try to cram everything from the chapter onto the chart. Then, you can quickly review. Put page numbers after your phrases so that you can very quickly look back to refresh your memory on an item.

5. Reflection will enrich your understanding of the material and involve you actively in the text. For example, consider the following:
   - Imagine yourself as an immigrant traveling west by train and settling. What would you write to your relatives back home about your trip?
   - Imagine yourself as a Native American or Mexican overhearing a Fourth of July speaker praising the American farmer for winning and settling an empty, untamed West. How would you reply?
   - Consider all the various stereotyped images of the West you have gained from books, television, or movies. How would you revise those images after reading this chapter?

RECITE/REVIEW

REVIEW QUESTIONS: This section has a sampling of multiple choice, short essay, and extended essay questions that you should be able to answer when you have completed the chapter and used other study techniques. To help you in reviewing the material, questions have been grouped according to the major sections of the chapter. Of course, you cannot expect your tests to be set up in this way.

▶ AMERICAN COMMUNITIES ◀

Multiple Choice

1. Which one of the following groups was NOT part of the pressure to reduce and reorganize the Indian Territory of the Five Civilized Tribes?
   - a. other Indian groups
   - b. boomers
   - c. miners
   - d. African Americans

2. This act dissolved Indian Territory and sovereign status that the Five Tribes did not regain until 1977:
   - a. Curtis Act.
   - b. Morrill Act.
   - c. Dawes Act.
   - d. Caminetti Act.

Map Question

3. No Man's Land was located in
   - a. western Oklahoma.
   - b. the eastern Dakotas.
   - c. northern Kansas.
   - d. central Wyoming.

▶ INDIAN PEOPLE UNDER SIEGE ◀

Multiple Choice

4. At the close of the Civil War, the majority of Indians in the trans-Mississippi West lived in
   - a. the Southwest.
   - b. Texas.
   - c. the Great Plains.
   - d. Indian Territory.

5. As an example of settler pressure, this part of Indian Territory was abolished and opened to white settlement in 1854:
   - a. Kansas and Nebraska.
   - b. North and South Dakota.
   - c. No Man's Land.
   - d. the Southwest.

6. The destruction of the buffalo and their way of life convinced many of these vision-seeking Great Plains people to conclude they could only fight or die:
   - a. Comanche.
   - b. Navajo.
   - c. Apache.
   - d. Lakota.

7. Which one of the following was the original leader of the Nez Percé tribe?
   - a. Cochise.
   - b. Geronimo.
   - c. Chief Joseph.
   - d. Old Chief Tukekas.

Map Question

8. The conflict known as Greasy Grass or Little Bighorn took place in
   - a. Wyoming.
   - b. Montana.
   - c. South Dakota.
   - d. Nebraska.

Short Essay

9. Discuss how, in a sense, "Custer's Last Stand" was really a defeat for the Indians.

▶ THE INTERNAL EMPIRE ◀

Multiple Choice

10. Which one of the following has the LEAST to do with the others?
    a. *United States* v. *Reynolds*
    b. Sante Fe Ring
    c. Deseret
    d. Brigham Young

11. The Mormons learned how to survive in their area by relying on farming techniques learned from
    a. local Indian tribes.
    b. the newly-created Department of Agriculture.
    c. African Americans whose ancestors practiced it as an age-old art.
    d. Spanish priests.

12. The "Cortina War" is a good example of conflict over western expansion between
    a. open range ranchers and crop farmers who wanted fencing.
    b. striking miners and their employers.
    c. Mexican communities and Anglo farmer encroachment.
    d. California ranchers fighting each other over water rights.

13. Which one of the following is the RESULT of the other three?
    a. southwest territories become states
    b. land closure in the southwest
    c. Mexican women lose status in the community
    d. Mexicanos become primarily urban

Map Questions

14. In which one of the following states was silver NOT mined?
    a. Idaho
    b. Colorado
    c. California
    d. Arizona

15. Which one of the following statements is true?
    a. All Mormons settled in Utah.
    b. There were scattered Mormon settlements in California.
    c. Mormons settled no farther south than Arizona.
    d. All Mormon settlements were in the continental United States.

Short Essay

16. Why was the West called the "internal empire"?

Extended Essay

17. What were the short and long-term effects of mining on the West?

▶ THE CATTLE INDUSTRY ◀

Multiple Choice

18. Which one of the following was NOT a reason for the demise of the huge cattle barons by the late 1880s?
    a. overstocked herds that depleted the limited grass supply
    b. constant danger of Indian attack
    c. severe summer and winter weather in 1885–1887
    d. pressure to fence and regulate formerly open land

19. Which one of the following statements is true?
    a. Gunfights were common in cattle towns.
    b. Mexican and Indian cowboys were paid the same as African Americans.
    c. Sheep and cattle could not graze on the same land.
    d. Prostitution was legal in most western towns.

Short Essay

20. What factors worked against community stability in western cattle towns?

▶ FARMING COMMUNITIES ON THE PLAINS ◀

Multiple Choice

21. Which one of the following is NOT true of the Homestead Act of 1862?
    a. It was most successful in the central and upper Midwest.
    b. Big-time land speculators gained the most.
    c. A person could gain land by settling and improving it over five years.
    d. Most farmers gained their lands this way.

22. Which one of the following statements is true?
    a. Few European immigrants settled on the Great Plains.
    b. Most settlers on the Great Plains lived in compact communities.
    c. By 1900, one third of farmers did not own their land.
    d. Most farm families preferred bartering to using cash.

Short Essay

23. How did various members of a farm family spend their time?

Extended Essay

24. In what ways did the railroad change the lives and the habits of Midwesterners?

▶ THE WORLD'S BREADBASKET ◀

Multiple Choice

25. Technological improvements allowed the average farmer to produce up to THIS many more times than before:
    a. two.   c. 25.
    b. ten.   d. 50.

26. From Nebraska to California, this became the most prosperous crop in the late 1800s:
    a. rice.   c. corn.
    b. cotton.   d. wheat.

27. In what year did the National Reclamation Act take place?
    a. 1897   c. 1905
    b. 1902   d. 1907

28. Which one of the following species was the most beneficial to the grasslands of the Great Plains?
    a. antelope
    b. cattle
    c. buffalo
    d. horses

Map Question

29. In 1872, the first national park was established in
    a. the Grand Canyon.
    b. Sequoia.
    c. Yellowstone.
    d. Yosemite.

Short Essay

30. What is the connection between forests and water in the ecology of the West?

Extended Essay

31. What role did technology play in the evolution of farming from a family-based, labor-intensive activity into agribusiness?

▶ THE WESTERN LANDSCAPE ◀

Multiple Choice

32. These two people, who were actual westerners, staged and popularized the Wild West Show:
    a. Edward Zane Carroll Judson and Owen Wister.
    b. Nat Love and Calamity Jane.
    c. Frederic Remington and Charles Russell.
    d. Joseph McCoy and William Cody.

33. Which one of the following is NOT one of the accomplishments of Alice Cunningham Fletcher?
    a. She wrote the critical work *Century of Dishonor.*
    b. She helped support the Omaha Indians.
    c. She wrote a study on the status of Indian peoples.
    d. She was a pioneering ethnographer in studying Indian societies.

34. Which one of the following is the RESULT of the other three?
    a. Albert Bierstadt paints the Rocky Mountains
    b. fewer Indians in the Rocky Mountains
    c. Yellowstone National Park created
    d. *Ward* v. *Racehorse*

Short Essay

35. Contrast the image presented in the Wild West shows with the reality of life in the western frontier times.

Extended Essay

36. What effects did settlers have on the natural landscape of the West, and what effects did the natural landscape have on the settlers?

▶ THE TRANSFORMATION OF INDIAN SOCIETIES ◀

Multiple Choice

37. Which one of the following was the RESULT of the other three?
   a. Great Sioux War
   b. massacre at Wounded Knee
   c. popularity of the Ghost Dance
   d. Wovoka's vision

38. The Yahi are to California as the Flatheads are to
   a. Washington.
   b. Arizona.
   c. North Dakota.
   d. Montana.

39. The reformers' intentions in both the reservation policy and the Dawes Act was to
   a. protect Indian culture.
   b. curtail white settlement.
   c. assimilate tribes into white culture.
   d. get tribes to fight each other.

40. If you were a member of the largest Indian nation in the United States, surviving on sheep herding, weaving, and jewelry making, you were a
   a. Cheyenne.
   b. Ute.
   c. Navaho.
   d. Hopi.

Short Essay

41. Describe the relationships between the Indians and the various American religious groups during this time period.

Extended Essay

42. What were the provisions of the Dawes Severalty Act, and what were its long-term effects on the Indian tribes that lived in the United States?

▶CHRONOLOGY QUESTIONS◀

Multiple Choice

43. Which one of the following gives the correct chronological order of these events?
    (1) Forest Management Act   (3) Timber Culture Act
    (2) Morrill Act   (4) Dawes Severalty Act

    a. 2, 3, 4, 1   c. 4, 2, 3, 1
    b. 3, 2, 4, 1   d. 1, 2, 4, 3

44. The Census Bureau announced that the end of the frontier line happened in this year:
    a. 1870.   c. 1890.
    b. 1880.   d. 1900.

45. Which one of the following events did NOT occur in 1866?
    a. The Texas cattle drives begin.
    b. The reservation system is established in Medicine Lodge Treaty.
    c. Alaska is purchased.
    d. Yellowstone National Park is created.

46. From the beginning of the Texas cattle drives to the collapse of the cattle boom was a period of
    a. 16 years.
    b. 21 years.
    c. ten years.
    d. seven years.

ANSWERS–CHAPTER 18

American Communities
  1. c, pp. 530–531
  2. a, p. 531
  3. a, p. 531

Indian People Under Siege
  4. c, p. 532
  5. a, p. 533
  6. d, p. 535
  7. d, p. 537
  8. b, p. 533
  9. p. 536

The Internal Empire
  10. b, pp. 540–541
  11. a, p. 541
  12. c, p. 542
  13. c, pp. 541–542
  14. c, p. 538
  15. b, p. 540
  16. pp. 537, 543
  17. pp. 537–540

The Cattle Industry
  18. b, p. 545
  19. c, pp. 544–545
  20. p. 545

Farming Communities on the Plains
  21. d, pp. 545–546
  22. c, pp. 546–548
  23. p. 547
  24. pp. 546–547

The World's Breadbasket
  25. b, p. 549
  26. d, p. 550
  27. b, p. 552
  28. c, p. 551
  29. c, p. 552
  30. pp. 552–553
  31. pp. 549–550

The Western Landscape
  32. d, pp. 554–555
  33. a, p. 556
  34. b, pp. 553–554
  35. pp. 543–544, 554–555
  36. pp. 553–556

The Transformation of Indian Societies
  37. b, p. 558
  38. d, p. 559
  39. c, pp. 534, 557
  40. c, pp. 559–560
  41. p. 557
  42. pp. 557–561

Chronology Questions
  43. a, p. 560
  44. c, p. 560
  45. d, p. 560
  46. b, p. 560

Technology and Environment	
Technology That Allowed "Conquest" of the Area	**Environmental Impact of Settlement And Technologies Used★**
Mining	
Cattle Ranching	
Agriculture:	
a. Central and Upper Midwest	
b. Great Plains	
c. California	

★ Include any laws that were significant in either a positive or negative way.

CHAPTER 19

The Incorporation of America, 1865–1900

SURVEY

Chapter Overview: This chapter covers the industrialization of America from 1865 to 1900. This transformation was based on the railroads, which in turn encouraged other industries as well as the development of large-scale corporations. Labor unions organized on a national level to counter the size and power of the employers—but with mixed results. America also continued to urbanize with rapid growth of the cities, unplanned and residential patterns reflecting social class divisions. The South tried to participate in the growth as the New South but generally reinforced old patterns. Gospels of wealth and work reinforced differences between the rising middle class and the factory workers, but leisure-time activities such as sports added to national identity.

Before you begin reading, turn to the CHRONOLOGY at the end of the chapter. Review it to orient yourself in space and time and understand who the leading characters are in the story this chapter will tell. Look for cause and effect relationships. Note unfamiliar terms that you will be learning about. Use the tips and questions at the beginning of Chapter 17 of the Study Guide as a guide for your use of the time line. Return to the CHRONOLOGY after you have read the chapter to see how much you have learned.

QUESTIONS/READ

As you read each section, use the questions to help you focus on the major themes. Use them as a way to organize note-taking as you read. The objective is for you to be able to answer these questions after you have read the chapter and completed the study skills exercises. Be on the lookout for important terms that you should be able to identify (see the study skills section in Chapter 18 of the Study Guide for tips on how to fully identify these important terms), and do the map exercises as you go along.

AMERICAN COMMUNITIES:
- Summarize how the industrialization and urbanization of America affected community, and use Chicago, Illinois as a specific example of these changes. Follow this theme throughout the chapter.
- **Identify:** Packingtown, knife men, feedlots

THE RISE OF INDUSTRY, THE TRIUMPH OF BUSINESS:
- Describe the rapid industrialization and large-scale business organizations that characterized the economy, and discuss the gospel of wealth ideology that supported it.
- Explain how Thomas Alva Edison typified the revolution in technology.
- Trace the growth of mechanization and the expanding market for goods that accompanied it.
- **Identify:** Centennial Exposition of 1876, Montgomery Ward, Sears Roebuck, A&P, Woolworth, Marshall Field, Filene's, Macy's, vertical integration, horizontal combination,

Sherman Antitrust Act, Jay Gould, John Rockefeller, Andrew Carnegie, social Darwinism, Horatio Alger

- **Map exercise:** *Patterns of Industry, 1900:* (p. 568) Where was industrial manufacturing concentrated in 1900? What states were the major sources of materials such as iron ore and coal?

LABOR IN THE AGE OF BIG BUSINESS:

- Discuss the effects that dramatic economic change had on labor and labor organizations.
- Compare the gospel of wealth and the gospel of work.
- **Identify:** George McNeil, Frederick Winslow Taylor, greenhands, outwork, Chinese Exclusion Act, Knights of Labor, ladies assemblies, Leonora Barry, eight-hour leagues, Haymarket Square incident, the American Federation of Labor, Samuel Gompers, Labor Day

THE NEW SOUTH:

- Explain the concept of the New South and why it did not materialize except in the Piedmont communities.
- Compare the South and the North in the industrial booms and in labor organization.
- **Identify:** Henry Woodfin Grady, a "New South," Red Shirts, Ellison Smyth, convict labor, good roads movement, a company town or mill village, customs of incorporation

THE INDUSTRIAL CITY:

- Outline the explosive growth of the cities as the economy expanded, including the various problems that developed from concentration of the population.
- Compare the new industrialization to the older manufacturing before the Civil War.
- Describe the effects of social class on the structures of cities.
- **Identify:** dumbbell, Fifth Avenue and other wealthy neighborhoods, Frederick Law Olmsted, Louis H. Sullivan, American Renaissance, John Roebling, suburbs, buffer zones
- **Map exercise:** *Population of Foreign Birth by Region, 1880:* (p. 581) Where did the majority of European immigrants settle in this period? Which area was affected the least? In what areas do you find French Canadians, Cubans, and Mexicans in 1880? Compare this map with the one on page 373 that shows similar information for 1860. What area has shown the greatest growth in immigrant population?

CULTURE AND SOCIETY IN THE GILDED AGE:

- Summarize the interests and issues in society and culture in the Gilded Age.
- Describe the life of the different classes of the Gilded Age and compare them to the pre-Civil War era.
- **Identify:** Mark Twain, Thorstein Veblen, "conspicuous consumption," "Diamond Jim" Brady, Newport, New York's Waldorf-Astoria hotel, H. H. Richardson, Carnegie, Harriet Spofford's *Art Decoration,* Chautauqua, gospel of exercise, *The Brownie Book, St. Nicholas, Little Women, Malbuerica, Ama Reka, Dollerica, barrios,* Young Men's and Young Women's Christian Associations, Tin Pan Alley, ragtime, Coney Island

CULTURE IN CONFLICT, CULTURE IN COMMON:

- Discuss how new leisure time helped build a greater sense of national identity and at the same time created more conflicts over control of parks and recreation areas.

- Describe how education differed based on gender, race and/or social class.
- **Identify:** kindergarten, Morrill Act, Johns Hopkins, Vassar, Women's Educational and Industrial Union, industrial education, Fisk, Booker T. Washington, Tuskegee, Forest Park/Tandy Park issue, blue laws, Scott Joplin, vaudeville, National pastime, Knickerbockers, National League, Albert Spaulding, Negro Leagues, Brotherhood of Professional Baseball Players, home team

CONCLUSION:
- Explain how industrialization and urbanization opened new worlds for rich and poor alike and what class problems remained.

REVIEW QUESTIONS: Use these to check your grasp of the major chapter themes. It is good practice to write out essay answers to these questions.

STUDY SKILLS EXERCISES

1. **Vocabulary:** To make vocabulary even more useful to you in studying, make sure you look at the entire sentence and understand the word in its context. Take the word "forte" below as an example. Do not just look up the word in a dictionary. How are the authors using the word? They are applying it here to Jay Gould, who was an example of a ruthless speculator who was talented at, and notorious for, questionable financial maneuvers.

monopoly, p. 566	aesthetic, p. 582
consolidation, p. 569	gilded, p. 584
financiers, p. 571	cosmopolitan, p. 587
forte, p. 571	philanthropists, p. 588
depressions, p. 574	cabarets, p. 590
amenable, p. 576	

2. Look at the chapter outline on page 565. Remember to make the arrangement of a textbook work for you. At the very minimum, you should be able to recognize or identify every term or name in the main headings and subheadings after you have read the chapter. Do not neglect looking at the title and making connections between the title and the outline. Evaluate the appropriateness of the chapter title after you are finished reading the chapter. Remember that the key to successful studying is to INTERACT with the text as much as possible.

3. When you look at each question in the headings under the QUESTIONS/READ section, remember that you need to read the total section to answer the questions adequately. You should imagine that you are explaining the answers to someone else. This forces you to consider how you would arrange your answers and what clarifying examples and illustrations you would use.

4. **Maps: Study Tip:** When you look at the maps or develop your own, you should reinforce your knowledge by asking yourself the importance of each location or piece of information on the maps. Why is this particular city, river, state, battle, or other location significant in this chapter? Following this practice is another way to interact with, reinforce, and review material. An assortment of blank maps are attached to the end of this study guide. You can photocopy them to practice map skills.

5. **Making Connections:** How did the conquest of the West prepare the way for the industrial age? (Chapters Eighteen and Nineteen)

6. **Reflection:** Imagine yourself as a person from a rural area coming to a city to find a job. What obstacles might you find and what possible successes would you have? Repeat this reflection as an African American and as a newly arrived immigrant from Eastern Europe.

RECITE/REVIEW

REVIEW QUESTIONS: This section has a sampling of multiple choice, short essay, and extended essay questions that you should be able to answer when you have completed the chapter and used other study techniques. To help you in reviewing the material, questions have been grouped according to the major sections of the chapter. Of course, you cannot expect your tests to be set up in this way.

▶ AMERICAN COMMUNITIES ◀

Multiple Choice

1. If you were a skilled worker in Packingtown, you were MOST likely to be
   a. Lithuanian.
   b. Scandanavian.
   c. German or Irish.
   d. Russian or Polish.

2. Which one of the following was NOT one of the elements that bound the Packingtown community to the national economic network?
   a. Chicago was a gateway city, or destination point for raw materials and exporter of products.
   b. Chicago meat-packer magnates exemplified monopoly capitalism.
   c. Huge factories had efficient production schedules.
   d. The most successful organized labor groups were there.

▶ RISE OF INDUSTRY, THE TRIUMPH OF BUSINESS ◀

Multiple Choice

3. Thomas Alva Edison's laboratory in Menlo Park, New Jersey was one of the first to be devoted to
   a. improving worker efficiency.
   b. industrial research.
   c. solving environmental problems.
   d. fighting diseases.

4. While there were many new inventions, the basis of industrial growth in the decades after the Civil War was
   a. mining.
   b. meat-packing.
   c. the railroad.
   d. textile manufacturing.

5. During the economic boom of the mid-to-late 1800s, the geographic center of manufacturing kept moving
   a. north.
   b. south.
   c. east.
   d. west.

6. The United Fruit Company was to vertical integration as THIS company was to horizontal combination:
   a. U.S. Steel.
   b. Sears and Roebuck.
   c. Standard Oil.
   d. American Tobacco.

7. Vertical integration is to the control of production of a product as horizontal combination is to control of
   a. the market for a product.
   c. the boards and financiers.
   b. the labor force.
   d. all raw materials.

8. Ironically, the Sherman Anti-Trust Act was interpreted by the courts to inhibit growth of THIS group rather than the industrial giants it was meant to control:
   a. city political machines.
   c. research labs.
   b. trade unions.
   d. banks.

9. Which one of the following would be LEAST likely to espouse the "gospel of wealth"?
   a. Russell Conwell
   c. Andrew Carnegie
   b. George McNeil
   d. Jay Gould

Map Question

10. In 1900 patterns of industry, you would find the MOST coal mining in these states:
    a. Washington, Oregon, Idaho, and Nevada.
    b. Illinois, Ohio, Kentucky, Michigan, and Iowa.
    c. Utah, Colorado, New Mexico, and Arizona.
    d. Alabama, Georgia, South Carolina and North Carolina.

11. In 1900, which one of the following was located from coast to coast?
    a. chief manufacturing cities
    c. iron and steel mills
    b. coal mining
    d. iron ore

Short Essay

12. Who were the winners and the losers of the "Incorporation of America"?

13. Describe the changes in marketing and merchandising that occurred in post-Civil War America.

Extended Essay

14. Compare and contrast Rockefeller's and Carnegie's rise to commercial dominance in their respective fields.

Multiple Choice

15. In 1883, a year of "minor" recession, this percentage of industrial workers in America lived below the poverty line:
    a. 10.
    b. 25.
    c. 40.
    d. 50.

16. Which one of the following unions had the LEAST in common with the other three?
    a. American Federation of Labor
    b. Eight-Hour League
    c. Our Girls Co-operative Manufacturing Co.
    d. Knights of Labor

17. The violence in the Haymarket Square incident was an example of
    a. the turmoil in the urban ghettos.
    b. racial tensions between African Americans and new European immigrants.
    c. hostilities that broke out in large crowds at sporting events.
    d. hostility to labor union organizing.

18. Which one of the following statements is true?
    a. Most workers belonged to labor unions.
    b. By the end of the nineteenth century, two thirds of Americans were wage workers.
    c. Most wage earners worked for large companies.
    d. The outwork system was completely obsolete in the garment industry.

Short Essay

19. The unionization movement harmed whom?

Extended Essay

20. Explain how the growth of industry affected different groups, including farm workers, immigrants, women, and minorities.

▶ THE NEW SOUTH ◀

Multiple Choice

21. Which one of the following was NOT a factor that held back southern progress after the Civil War?
    a. lack of investment capital and banks
    b. reliance on the cotton industry
    c. lack of natural resources
    d. segregation of the workforce

22. Which one of the following statements is NOT true?
    a. African American men were mostly limited to unskilled jobs.
    b. Most African American women worked in domestic service.
    c. Labor unions were generally segregated.
    d. Immigrants made up a significant portion of the southern industrial workforce.

23. The percentage of southern mill workers who were under 16 was
    a. 10.
    b. 25.
    c. 33.
    d. 5.

Short Essay

24. Describe the transformation of the Piedmont region after the Civil War.

▶ THE INDUSTRIAL CITY ◀

Multiple Choice

25. By 1890, what fraction of Americans were city dwellers?
    a. one fifth
    b. one fourth
    c. one third
    d. one half

26. Which one of the following contributed LEAST to the growth of cities after the Civil War?
    a. expansion of the railroad
    b. migration of African Americans from rural areas
    c. young white men moving from farms
    d. immigration from eastern and southern Europe

27. Which one of the following groups was LEAST likely to return to their native lands after immigrating to America?
    a. Russian Jews
    b. Italians
    c. Greeks
    d. Serbians

Map Questions

28. Very few of the immigrants in the 1880s went to this region of the United States:
    a. the South.
    c. the Northeast.
    b. the Pacific Coast.
    d. the Southwest.

29. Which one of the following groups is not correctly matched with the region where they settled?
    a. Chinese/California
    b. Mexicans/Texas
    c. Cubans/Florida
    d. French Canadians/Minnesota

Short Essay

30. Describe the role that architects played in the City Beautiful movement.

Extended Essay

31. How did the growth of cities impact the environment?

▶ CULTURE AND SOCIETY IN THE GILDED AGE ◀

Multiple Choice

32. The new style of spending of the rich was labeled THIS by sociologist Thorstein Veblen:
    a. customs of incorporation.
    c. the Gilded Age.
    b. conspicuous consumption.
    d. gospel of wealth.

33. When the owners of fancy hotels and gambling houses realized that entertainment for the masses could pay, they opened a/an
    a. baseball stadium.
    c. vaudeville theater.
    b. race track.
    d. amusement park.

34. Which one of the following was a new member of the middle class late in the nineteenth century?
    a. small business owner
    c. engineer
    b. lawyer
    d. teacher

Short Essay

35. Why did immigrants tend to cluster with people of similar ethnic backgrounds?

Extended Essay

36. Describe how the "Gospel of Wealth" could be used as a justification for "Conspicuous Consumption."

▶ CULTURES IN CONFLICT, CULTURE IN COMMON ◀

Multiple Choice

37. Which one of the following is NOT correctly matched to his accomplishment(s)?
    a. Louis Sullivan/skyscraper architect
    b. Booker T. Washington/Tuskegee founder and educator
    c. Henry W. Grady/*Atlanta Constitution* editor
    d. John Roebling/baseball and sports entrepreneur

38. Which one of the following was NOT a trend in post-Civil War education?
    a. growth of kindergartens
    b. half of all children attended high school
    c. establishment of women's colleges
    d. emphasis on vocational training for immigrants

39. Which one of the following was designed to appeal primarily to the middle class?
    a. public playgrounds   c. public tennis courts
    b. beer gardens open on Sunday   d. picnicking in city parks

Short Essay

40. What elements of American life brought different ethnic groups together?

41. Describe the growth of educational opportunities for women of all classes after the Civil War.

Extended Essay

42. Why does it seem reasonable that enthusiasm for sports and other forms of entertainment would have become so great during the "Gilded Age"?

▶ CHRONOLOGY QUESTIONS ◀

Multiple Choice

43. Which one of the following events did NOT occur in 1882?
    a. Nineteenth-century immigration to the United States peaks at 1.2 million.
    b. The Sherman Antitrust Act is passed.
    c. Congress passes the Chinese Exclusion Act.
    d. Standard Oil Trust is founded.

44. Severe depressions occurred in
    a. 1873 and 1893.
    b. 1870 and 1890.
    c. 1881 and 1891.
    d. 1866 and 1896.

45. Which one of the following lists the correct chronological order of events?
    (1) Tuskegee Institute founded
    (2) Sherman Antitrust Act passed
    (3) lightbulb invented
    (4) Haymarket Riot

    a. 3, 2, 1, 4
    b. 1, 3, 2, 4
    c. 3, 1, 4, 2
    d. 2, 3, 1, 4

46. Which one of the following events did NOT occur after the Civil War?
    a. telephone patented
    b. rural free mail delivery
    c. Morrill Act
    d. National Baseball League founded

ANSWERS-CHAPTER 19

American Communities
   1. c, p. 565
   2. d, p. 566

Rise of Industry, The Triumph of Business
   3. b, p. 567
   4. c, p. 568
   5. d, p. 568
   6. c, p. 571
   7. a, p. 571
   8. b, p. 571
   9. b, pp. 571–572
   10. b, p. 568
   11. c, p. 568
   12. pp. 567–572
   13. pp. 569–570
   14. pp. 571–572

Labor in the Age of Big Business
   15. c, p. 574
   16. a, pp. 574–576
   17. d, p. 575
   18. b, pp. 572–573
   19. pp. 574–576
   20. pp. 573–574

The New South
   21. c, pp. 576–577
   22. d, p. 577
   23. b, p. 578
   24. pp. 578–579

The Industrial City
   25. c, p. 579
   26. c, pp. 579–580
   27. a, p. 580
   28. a, p. 581
   29. d, p. 581
   30. p. 582
   31. p. 583

Culture and Society in the Gilded Age
   32. b, p. 584
   33. d, p. 587
   34. c, p. 584
   35. pp. 586–587
   36. pp. 571, 584

Cultures in Conflict, Culture in Common
   37. d, pp. 576, 582, 589
   38. b, pp. 588–589
   39. c, pp. 589–590
   40. pp. 587, 589–592
   41. p. 588
   42. pp. 590–592

Chronology Questions
   43. b, p. 591
   44. a, p. 591
   45. c, p. 591
   46. c, p. 591

CHAPTER 20
Commonwealth and Empire, 1870–1900

SURVEY

Chapter Overview: This chapter covers the conflicts between the populists and those groups that held the wealth and power. Mass political movements of farmers and workers were organized. These movements were also actively supported and shaped by women, who were also struggling for their own rights. There was a moment of democratic promise that was lost when Americans might have established a commonwealth based on agreement of the people for the common good. Instead, a national governing class and a large bureaucratic state emerged. While debating their future, most Americans seemed united in pursuing an empire. Anti-imperialists lost as the United States acquired numerous territories and took an interventionist stance toward others.

Before you begin reading, turn to the CHRONOLOGY at the end of the chapter. Review it to orient yourself in space and time and understand who the leading characters are in the story this chapter will tell. Look for cause and effect relationships. Note unfamiliar terms that you will be learning about. Use the tips and questions at the beginning of Chapter 17 of the Study Guide as a guide for your use of the time line. Return to the CHRONOLOGY after you have read the chapter to see how much you have learned.

QUESTIONS/READ

As you read each section, use the questions to help you focus on the major themes. Use them as a way to organize note-taking as you read. The objective is for you to be able to answer these questions after you have read the chapter and completed the study skills exercises. Be on the lookout for important terms that you should be able to identify (see the study skills section in Chapter 18 of the Study Guide for tips on how to fully identify these important terms), and do the map exercises as you go along.

AMERICAN COMMUNITIES:
- Explain the meaning of "a moment of democratic promise" as envisioned by Edward Bellamy and his followers in Point Loma, California as well as other reformers and populist organizers. Carry this theme throughout the chapter.
- **Identify:** Edward Bellamy's *Looking Backward* and his sequel novel *Equality*, industrial army, "new nation," Point Loma, California, Katjerome Tingley

TOWARD A NATIONAL GOVERNING CLASS:
- Describe the effects of the rapid expansion of government that paralleled the rapid growth of the economy in the late nineteenth century.
- Outline the type of record or principles each political party presented and relate them to the emergence of a national governing class.
- **Identify:** Interstate Commerce Commission, boodle, spoils, John Jay Chapman, James Garfield, the Pendleton Act, Circuit Court of Appeals Act of 1891

FARMERS AND WORKERS ORGANIZE THEIR COMMUNITIES:

- Describe the alternative governmental system as viewed by the Populist movement.
- Compare the roles of farmers, urban workers, women, and African Americans in the Populist movement.
- **Identify:** Grange, Oliver H. Kelley, thieves in the night, *Munn* v. *Illinois,* Charles W. Macune, National Farmers' Alliance and Industrial Union, national Colored Farmers' Alliance and Cooperative Union, Southern and Northern Farmers' Alliance, Tompkins Square Riot and the Great Uprising of 1877, Law and Order League, National Guard, Progress and Poverty, Henry George, Frances E. Willard, WCTU, Leonora M. Barry, Mary E. Lease, *Farmer's Wife,* Annie Diggs, People's Party Platform, Ignatius Donnelly, "pepper and salt"
- **Map exercise:** *Strikes by State, 1880:* (p. 606) What three states had the greatest number of strikes after the uprising of 1877? Which five states had the second highest rate? Where were most of these strikes concentrated? What general areas had the least number of strikes?

THE CRISIS OF THE 1890s:

- Discuss the crisis of the 1890s and the effects it had on people's view of the political system.
- **Identify:** Ignatius Donnelly, *Caesar's Column,* Philadelphia and Reading Railroad, vagrancy laws, Jacob Sechler Coxey, the Homestead strike, the Pullman strike, Amalgamated Iron, Steel and Tin Workers, Henry C. Frick, George Pullman, Eugene V. Debs, American Railway Union, social gospel movement, W. D. P. Bliss, Washington Gladden, *Applied Christianity,* Beulahland, *If Christ Came to Chicago, If Jesus Came to Boston, In His Steps, Rerum Novarum,* Young Women's Christian Association

POLITICS OF REFORM, POLITICS OF ORDER:

- Explain why the election of 1896 was a turning point in American politics.
- Outline the free silver issue and the positions taken by the political parties.
- Trace the ways in which the rights of African Americans were eroded after Reconstruction.
- **Identify:** "soft" currency, greenbacks, 1873 Coinage Act, Sherman Silver Purchase Act, McKinley Tariff, Silver Democrats, William McKinley, William Jennings Bryan, David Waite, "Cross of Gold" speech, Democratic-Populist ticket, Ida B. Wells, American Protective Association, Jim Crow laws, Civil Rights Cases, *Plessy* v. *Ferguson, Cumming* v. *Richmond County Board of Education,* grandfather clauses, *Red Record,* National Association of Colored Women, Tom Watson
- **Map exercise:** *Election of 1896, by States:* (p. 614) What areas of the country did each candidate carry? What types of areas were they? Notice that the popular vote was not that far apart for both candidates but the electoral vote was. Why was that?

THE IMPERIALISM OF RIGHTEOUSNESS:

- Summarize the interests and issues that persuaded many Americans of the need for an overseas empire.
- **Identify:** Albert J. Beveridg, the white man's burden, Frederick Jackson Turner, World's Fair in Chicago, Frederick Douglass's and Ida B. Wells's views on the World's Fair, Josiah Strong, "army, navy, and the 'Y,'" William H. Seward, Alfred Thayer Mahan, *The Influence of Sea Power upon History, 1660–1873,* Secretaries of State James Blaine and John Hay, American lake, Good Neighbor Policy, Pan-American Conference, Great White Fleet, Naval War College, Liliuokalani, ocean bride, Open Door, Boxer Rebellion

- **Map exercise:** *The American Domain:* (p. 619) In what two general areas was the United States involved? Be able to locate Cuba, Puerto Rico, Alaska, Hawaii, Guam, Midway, and the Philippines.

THE SPANISH-AMERICAN WAR:

- Outline the steps by which the United States gained an empire and developed a foreign policy for that empire. Draw on material from throughout the chapter.
- Discuss the causes and results of the Spanish-American War, including follow-up military actions.
- Summarize the arguments of the anti-imperialists.
- **Identify:** José Marti, *Maine,* Teller Amendment, a "splendid little war," Rough Riders, Platt Amendment, Cuban-American Treaty of 1903, Puerto Rico, Virgin Islands, Guam, Strong's Expansion, Theodore Roosevelt, George Dewey, Emilio Aquinaldo, *"gu-gus,"* the Anti-Imperialist League
- **Map exercise:** *The Spanish-American War:* (p. 622) What were the two theaters of action in the war? The war was largely a naval operation. What two water bodies were involved? Be able to locate Manila, and Santiago.

CONCLUSION:

- Describe what happened to the populists' desire to retain community self-government.

REVIEW QUESTIONS: Use these to check your grasp of the major chapter themes. It is good practice to write out essay answers to these questions.

STUDY SKILLS EXERCISES

1. **Vocabulary:** In the vocabulary list below is the word *commonwealth*. Remember, if you are not sure what these words mean, look them up. One meaning of the word *commonwealth* is a republic or a state founded and united by compact or agreement of the people for the common good or the commonwealth, the general welfare. How did this sense of community clash with imperialism as America expanded at home and overseas? Who was included and who was left out of the commonwealth? Include any relevant information from chapters Seventeen to Nineteen.

   commonwealth, p. 598   socialism, p. 610
   utopia, p. 598   egalitarian, p. 616
   partisans, p. 601   annexation, p. 620
   suffrage, p. 602   guerilla, p. 624
   solidarity, p. 607

2. Make a chart on the money question. It should be a two-column chart with the gold standard or hard money issue in one column and the silver standard or soft money in the other. Your topics to consider for each issue could be items such as the basis of each system, the advantages and disadvantages, political issues related to them, groups in favor and groups against, significant election results, laws that were passed, and outcome of the issue by 1900. You will find a sample blank at the end of this chapter.

3. **Making connections:** Be alert to making connections between chapters. The authors of your text always have a sentence in their conclusion section that ties into the next chapter. In addition, you are given sample essay questions in this review guide that point out connections. Make this work for you when studying. Your professor may have essay questions on the test

that require you to synthesize information across chapters. You must be alert yourself to connections since not all of the possibilities could be included in the study guide.

Notice that Chapters Eighteen, Nineteen, and Twenty all cover the same time period. Some common themes are the economic growth of America as well as arguments about what was best for America. Would all Americans be included? Here is an example of a question your instructor might ask: To what extent were all Americans included in the economic boom and growth from 1860 to 1900? Include a consideration of groups excluded and what steps they tried to take to change things.

How well was America fulfilling its democratic promise? If your course starts with Chapter Seventeen on Reconstruction, be sure to include this in your connection making.

Chapters Nineteen and Twenty: Compare the gospel of wealth to the social gospel.

4. **Reflections:**
   a. Imagine a debate between imperialists and anti-imperialists. What points would each side make? For further ideas, take specific individual parts as Josiah Strong, Ida Wells, Emilio Equinaldo, and Samuel Gompers.
   b. Imagine how Edward Bellamy would react if he "reappeared" here in the early twenty-first century. What do you think he would say? How would Ignatius Donnelly react to Bellamy or the 21st Century?

RECITE/REVIEW

REVIEW QUESTIONS: This section has a sampling of multiple choice, short essay, and extended essay questions that you should be able to answer when you have completed the chapter and used other study techniques. To help you in reviewing the material, questions have been grouped according to the major sections of the chapter. Of course, you cannot expect your tests to be set up in this way.

▶ AMERICAN COMMUNITIES ◀

Multiple Choice

1. Which one of the following was NOT one of Edward Bellamy's concepts in his novel *Looking Backward?*
   a. Automated machinery will eliminate most menial tasks.
   b. The United States would be a cooperative commonwealth.
   c. Communities collectively own businesses.
   d. The workday would be eight hours long.

2. The Point Loma community actually tried to create Bellamy's community ideas and
   a. managed to survive into the 1950s.
   b. failed within the first year.
   c. were not able to fulfill their children's education.
   d. were destroyed by rioters who considered them anarchists.

3. Bellamy hoped citizens would mobilize nationwide and
   a. establish cooperative communities throughout the world.
   b. overturn the existing political and economic leadership.
   c. work against the building of empire.
   d. create an international union.

Multiple Choice

4. Which one of the following was NOT a federal agency or department that grew or began during the period from 1870 to 1900?
    a. Treasury
    b. Veterans Bureau
    c. Labor
    d. Defense

5. From 1877 to 1893, the position of president of the United States was basically
    a. a weak position, yielding to Congress and state legislatures.
    b. a powerful position, directing Congress and the Courts.
    c. powerful in foreign policy but weak in domestic affairs.
    d. well established as a position of representing the "forgotten American."

6. The Pendleton Reform Act attempted to reform what area?
    a. civil rights
    b. railroad rates
    c. civil service
    d. public education

Short Essay

7. Why did citizens in the North and South hold differing views on the use of tariffs?

► FARMERS AND WORKERS ORGANIZE THEIR COMMUNITIES ◄

Multiple Choice

8. Which one of the following groups would be the LEAST likely to have many populists in it?
    a. farmers
    b. business executives
    c. workers
    d. African Americans

9. Which one of the following would NOT be in a Granger's list of "thieves in the night"?
    a. railroads
    b. farm equipment manufacturers
    c. banks
    d. labor unions

10. The Tompkins Square Riot and the Great Uprising of 1877 were both examples of reactions by
    a. white laborers against African Americans and foreigners.
    b. laborers demanding rights during the economic panic.
    c. National Guard soldiers against urban rioters.
    d. nationwide farmer alliances against big business and big government.

11. If you were a member of the largest organization of women in the world in the late nineteenth century, you would belong to the
    a. Women's Christian Temperance Union.
    b. Women's Union Missionary Society of Americans for Heathen Lands.
    c. National American Woman Suffrage Association.
    d. Young Women's Christian Association.

12. The People's Party, or Populists, ran the strongest in the 1892 election in this area of the country:
    a. New England.
    b. the Upper South.
    c. the Great Plains and the West.
    d. the Midwest.

Map Question

13. Which one of the following states is NOT one of those with the highest strike rates in 1880?
    a. Ohio
    c. New York
    b. Florida
    d. Pennsylvania

Short Essay

14. Compare the role of women in the labor and farmers' protest movements.

15. Describe the founding of the Populist Party and its role in the election of 1892.

Extended Essay

16. Compare the grievances of farmers and urban workers in the late nineteenth century.

▶ THE CRISIS OF THE 1890s ◀

Multiple Choice

17. The financial collapse and depression of the 1890s was precipitated by the downfall of this company in March 1893:
    a. U.S. Steel.
    b. Standard Oil Refineries.
    c. Union Pacific Railroad.
    d. Philadelphia and Reading Railroad.

18. In 1894, Jacob Coxey gathered an army. The members were
    a. part of Bellamy's concept of an industrial army.
    b. demanding a public works program to create jobs.
    c. women who were going to storm saloons to enforce prohibition.
    d. amalgamated strikers who were planning to storm Carnegie Steel.

Short Essay

19. What was the social gospel and who were its main leaders and followers?

▶ POLITICS OF REFORM, POLITICS OF ORDER ◀

Multiple Choice

20. If you were in favor of soft currency in the 1890s, you would be LEAST likely to support
    a. the gold standard.   c. free coinage of silver.
    b. treasury notes.   d. inflated currency.

21. If you believed in the promise of "a full dinner pail" in the 1900 election, then you voted for
    a. William Jennings Bryan.
    b. Tom Watson.
    c. William McKinley.
    d. Grover Cleveland.

22. Which one of the following was designed to help poor white southerners vote?
    a. literacy tests
    b. poll taxes
    c. grandfather clause
    d. *Plessy* v. *Ferguson*

23. Both nativism and Jim Crow laws were based on
    a. belief in white supremacy.
    b. antiimmigrant feelings.
    c. support of social equality.
    d. legal inferiority of African Americans.

24. Which one of the following is NOT true of the election of 1896?
    a. Conservatives triumphed over populism.
    b. Backing free silver was sufficient for victory.
    c. Republicans outspent Democrats and Populists combined.
    d. It was the most important election since Reconstruction.

Map Question

25. William Jennings Bryan won the most support in these states in the 1896 election:
    a. New England.
    b. the Midwest.
    c. the West and South.
    d. the Northeast.

Short Essay

26. Describe Bryan's "Free Silver" campaign.

Extended Essay

27. Why was organized labor nativistic?

▶ "IMPERIALISM OF RIGHTEOUSNESS" ◀

Multiple Choice

28. Which one of the following was NOT a cause of the financial crisis of 1893–1897?
   a. collapse of the railroads
   b. overbuilt economy
   c. conspicuous consumption
   d. limited size of domestic market

29. The Chicago World's Fair's promoted all of the following EXCEPT
   a. world-wide markets for American farm machinery.
   b. easier commercial and tourist travel to the Pacific.
   c. the material advantages of white civilization.
   d. equal partnership between the United States and Asia.

30. The Good Neighbor policy referred to
   a. Canada's desire to become part of the United States.
   b. trade agreements between the United States and Mexico.
   c. Hawaiian sugar plantations becoming dominated by Americans.
   d. American missionaries going to China.

31. Which one of the following was LEAST in favor of the annexation of Hawaii?
   a. James Blaine   c. Grover Cleveland
   b. Sanford Dole   d. William McKinley

Map Question

32. Which one of the following was connected to the purchase of Alaska?
   a. Guam   c. Philippines
   b. Hawaiian Islands   d. Aleutian Islands

Short Essay

33. What was the "White Man's Burden"?

Extended Essay

34. In what ways did economic concerns drive American imperialism?

35. In what ways did religious fervor drive American imperialism?

▶ THE SPANISH-AMERICAN WAR ◀

Multiple Choice

36. Which one of the following authors is NOT correctly matched to his book?
    a. Washington Gladden/*Applied Christianity*
    b. F. J. Turner/*The Significance of the Frontier in American History*
    c. Josiah Strong/*Expansion*
    d. George Dewey/*The Influence of Sea Power upon History*

37. Which one of the following is NOT an area of empire gained by the United States up to and including the McKinley administration?
    a. Panama Canal
    b. Philippines
    c. Hawaii
    d. Puerto Rico

38. Both the Teller and Platt Amendments illustrate the conflict of Americans over
    a. recognizing unions.
    b. allowing any foreign trade and overseas investment.
    c. acquiring empire—in this case Cuba.
    d. various Populist issues.

Map Question

39. Which one of the following is NOT the location of a battle in Cuba?
    a. Santiago Harbor
    b. Manila Bay
    c. San Juan Hill
    d. El Caney

Short Essay

40. Explain why the Philippine rebels shifted from fighting with the United States to fighting against it.

Extended Essay

41. In what ways did American expansion run counter to the country's founding ideals?

▶ CHRONOLOGY QUESTIONS ◀

Multiple Choice

42. Which one of the following is the CORRECT order for these events?

(1) McKinley re-elected   (3) Pendleton Civil Service Reform
(2) Hawaii annexed   (4) Alaska purchased

a. 4, 3, 2, 1   c. 4, 2, 3, 1
b. 2, 4, 1, 3   d. 1, 2, 4, 3

43. Which one of the following is the CORRECT order for these labor events?
    (1) Coxey's Army marches   (3) Tompkins Square Riot
    (2) Great Uprising of 1877   (4) Homestead steelworkers strike

    a. 2, 1, 4, 3   c. 4, 1, 3, 2
    b. 1, 4, 2, 3   d. 3, 2, 4, 1

44. *Plessy* v. *Ferguson* establishes segregation as "separate but equal" in
    a. 1876.   c. 1896.
    b. 1888.   d. 1899.

45. Which one of the following events did NOT happen in 1890?
    a. Sherman Silver Purchase Act
    b. financial panic and depression
    c. McKinley tariff enacted
    d. National American Woman Suffrage Association formed

46. Which one of the following is true?
    a. Hawaii was annexed during the Spanish-American War.
    b. Hawaii was annexed during Grover Cleveland's administration.
    c. The Dingley tariff followed Hawaiian annexation.
    d. Hawaii was annexed before William McKinley became president.

ANSWERS–CHAPTER 20

American Communities
1. d, p. 598
2. a, p. 599
3. b, p. 598

Toward A National Governing Class
4. d, p. 600
5. a, p. 601
6. c, p. 602
7. p. 601

Farmers and Workers Organize Their Communities
8. b, pp. 604–608
9. d, pp. 603–604
10. b, p. 605
11. a, p. 607
12. c, p. 608
13. b, p. 606
14. pp. 606–607
15. pp. 607–608
16. pp. 603–606

The Crisis of the 1890s
17. d, p. 608
18. b, p. 608
19. p. 611

Politics of Reform, Politics of Order
20. a, p. 612
21. c, p. 614
22. c, p. 615
23. a, pp. 614–615
24. b, pp. 612–614
25. c, p. 614
26. p. 612
27. p. 614

"Imperialism of Righteousness"
28. c, p. 616
29. d, p. 617
30. b, pp. 619–620
31. c, pp. 619–620
32. d, p. 619
33. pp. 616–617
34. pp. 618–621
35. pp. 617–618

The Spanish-American War
36. d, pp. 611, 616, 620, 624
37. a, pp. 620–624
38. c, pp. 622–623
39. b, p. 622
40. pp. 623–624
41. pp. 624–626

Chronology Questions
42. a, p. 625
43. d, p. 625
44. c, p. 625
45. b, p. 525
46. a, p. 625

Basis of the System	Gold Standard or Hard Money	Silver Standard or Soft Money
Advantages		
Disadvantages		
Related Political Issues		
Groups in Favor		
Groups Against		
Significant Election Results		
Laws Passed		
Outcome of Issue By 1900		

SURVEY

Chapter Overview: This chapter covers continued urbanization of America and the social problems that resulted from rapid unplanned growth of the cities. Both political bosses and reformers tried to respond to the reality of industrialized and urbanized America. Social Darwinism was challenged by the progressives who had a new, sometimes inconsistent, vision of the American community. They viewed the government as an ally to achieve realistic and pragmatic reforms. The climate for reform came from social workers, social scientists at universities, and investigative journalists. Both political parties would embrace progressive views. Presidents Roosevelt, Taft, and Wilson based their programs on these new ideas. Although much was accomplished, the progressive movement lacked unity and failed to address issues of class, race, or gender adequately. Legislation was not always enforced or had unintended negative consequences. In the long run, politics was affected by the demand for social justice, and attempts were made to confront the problems of rapid industrialization and urbanization.

Before you begin reading, turn to the CHRONOLOGY at the end of the chapter. Review it to orient yourself in space and time and understand who the leading characters are in the story this chapter will tell. Look for cause and effect relationships. Note unfamiliar terms that you will be learning about. Use the tips and questions at the beginning of Chapter 17 of the Study Guide as a guide for your use of the time line. Return to the CHRONOLOGY after you have read the chapter to see how much you have learned.

QUESTIONS/READ

As you read each section, use the questions to help you focus on the major themes. Use them as a way to organize note-taking as you read. The objective is for you to be able to answer these questions after you have read the chapter and completed the study skills exercises. Be on the lookout for important terms that you should be able to identify (see the study skills section in Chapter 18 of the Study Guide for tips on how to fully identify these important terms), and do the map exercises as you go along.

AMERICAN COMMUNITIES:
- Trace the process by which the women settlement house workers first began and the community of reform they tried to create.
- **Identify:** Henry Street Settlement House, Lillian Wald, Jane Addams, National Association for the Advancement of Colored People, "The whole world is my neighborhood"

THE CURRENTS OF PROGRESSIVISM:
- Summarize the principles of the progressives, the views of its principal proponents in journalism, social sciences, and government, and its legacy.
- Compare the themes and focus of progressivism at the local, state, and national level.

- **Identify:** Jane Addams, Hull House, subjective necessity, *Hull House Maps and Papers,* Florence Kelley, Lillian Wald, George W. Plunkitt, Timothy Sullivan, machine politics, Samuel Jones and Thomas L. Johnson, National Municipal League, Wisconsin Idea, initiative, referendum, direct primary, recall, muckrakers, Jacob Riis, S. S. McClure, Lincoln Steffens, Ida Tarbell, Ray Stannard Baker, exposure journalism, Meat Inspection Act, Pure Food and Drug Act, Lester Frank Ward, social Darwinism, John Dewey, John Commons, Richard Ely, the Fourteenth Amendment, Oliver Wendel Holmes, Louis Brandeis, social sciences, telic, genetic, *Gemeinschaft, Gesellschaft, ethical elite,* embryonic communities, *Lochner* v. *New York,* sociological jurisprudence, *Muller* v. *Oregon,* Brandeis Brief, Edward Ross

SOCIAL CONTROL AND ITS LIMITS:
- Discuss the aims of and problems with social control legislation desired by the progressives.
- **Identify:** Eugenics, the WCTU and the Anti-Saloon League, prohibition, pietist vs. ritualist issue, the social evil, Charles K. Parkhurst, white slave, Mann Act, Frederick C. Howe, nickelodeon, movie palace, National Board of Censorship, Elwood Cubberley, National Education Association report of 1918, Smith-Hughes Act of 1917, College Entrance Examination Board, E. L. Thorndike

WORKING-CLASS COMMUNITIES AND PROTEST:
- Outline the types of working-class communities, their problems, and the attempts to solve them through unions and reform legislation.
- Describe the role of immigrants in working-class communities.
- **Identify:** chains, Issei, Nisei, barrios, the uprising of the 20,000, the Triangle Shirtwaist Company fire, piece-rate system, Women's Trade Union League, ILGWU, Clara Lemlich, Pauline Newman, Rose Schneiderman, company town, scientific management, "slowing down" or "soldiering," Ludlow Massacre, AFL—a "union, pure and simple," Gompers, United Mine Workers, National Association of Manufacturers, "open shop," *Loewe* v. *Lawler,* secondary boycott, IWW—"one big union," William Haywood, "Bread and Roses" strike, McNamara Brothers, bohemian
- **Map/chart exercise:** *Immigration, 1900–1920:* (p. 644) Where did most immigrants to the United States come from in the years between 1900 and 1920? How did this compare to the nineteenth century? What percent of the American labor force was made up of foreign-born workers? What specific European countries ranked in the top four?

WOMEN'S MOVEMENTS AND BLACK AWAKENING:
- Summarize the role of women in the reform campaigns and the effects the campaigns had on women's participation in public life and leadership positions.
- Summarize the difficulties of black progressives in gaining recognition within the black community.
- **Identify:** General Federation of Women's Clubs, National Consumers League, white label, Florence Kelley, social housekeeping, Margaret Sanger, Booker T. Washington, Thomas Dixon's *The Clansman,* Tuskegee Institute, *Up from Slavery,* National Negro Business League, W. E. B. Du Bois, *A Red Record,* National Association of Colored Women, *The Souls of Black Folk,* "double consciousness," "talented tenth," Niagara Movement, NAACP, *The Crisis*

NATIONAL PROGRESSIVISM:

- Outline the attempts by both the Democratic and Republican parties to respond to demands that the governments, local, state, and national, address the issues of social justice.
- Describe how progressivism affected the office of the president.
- Discuss the candidates, issues, and outcome of the election of 1912.
- **Identify:** Theodore Roosevelt, bully pulpit, *Northern Securities* v. *United States,* Hepburn Act, Pure Food and Drug Act, Meat Inspection Act, trust-buster, preservation versus conservation, John Muir, Hetch Hetchy Valley, U.S. Forest Service, Gifford Pinchot, Yosemite Act of 1890, Sierra Club, National Park Service, Newlands Reclamation Act, Howard Taft, the Progressive Party, "New Nationalism" program, Square Deal, Woodrow Wilson, "New Freedom" program, Eugene V. Debs, Underwood Simmons Act, Sixteenth Amendment, Federal Reserve Act, Clayton Anti-Trust Act, Federal Trade Commission
- **Map exercises:** *The Establishment of National Parks and Forests* (p. 552) Review this map in Chapter 18 of the text. Which national parks and forests were established during Theodore Roosevelt's administration (1901–1908)?
  The Election of 1912: (p. 658) What was significant about Woodrow Wilson's election as a Democrat? What happened in the Republican Party that worked to Wilson's advantage? How did Teddy Roosevelt's popular and electoral vote compare to Taft's? How did Debs fare as a candidate? Look at the 1896 election map on page 614. What states that voted for Wilson might have voted for Taft (or for Roosevelt if he had been the Republican candidate)? What areas did Wilson carry that Bryan failed to in 1896?

CONCLUSION:

- Evaluate the legacy of the progressives.

REVIEW QUESTIONS: Use these to check your grasp of the major chapter themes. It is good practice to write out essay answers to these questions.

STUDY SKILLS EXERCISES:

1. Vocabulary:

rhetoric, p. 633	boycotts, p. 648
constituents, p. 635	bohemian, p. 649
dissident, p. 636	anarchist, p. 650
abysmal, p. 639	milieu, p. 651
parochial, p. 643	consecrate, p. 658

2. A chart that might be helpful in this chapter would be one in which you list the major writers, activists, and intellectuals down one side of the chart. Across the top, list major ideas, writings, positions held, and actions or organizations founded. A blank chart is attached to the end of this chapter.

You might also want to use a chart to help you compare the different kinds of immigrant communities described on pages 644–648. List the type of communities down the side, and then have columns for types of residents, living conditions, types of work, and any other factors you want to include.

3. Making connections:

- Modern-day political candidates, Republican, Democrat, and third party, like to invoke Theodore Roosevelt's name and somehow try to claim his legacy. Why do you think they pick Roosevelt so often?

- What was the connection between the social gospel and the progressive viewpoint?
- To what extent do we still debate many of the points of the Social Darwinists and Gospel of Wealth ideas versus the progressives and the Social Gospel?
- Analyze the possible connections between populism and progressivism as social reform movements. (Chapters Nineteen to Twenty-one)

4. **Reflection:** There are a number of debates that you could reflect on, and as you do, consider your own views on the subjects.
- Imagine a debate between Booker T. Washington and W. E. B. Du Bois. What issues would be discussed? What points would be made?
- Imagine a debate between Gifford Pinchot and John Muir. What issues would be discussed? What points would be made?

RECITE/REVIEW

REVIEW QUESTIONS: This section has a sampling of multiple choice, short essay, and extended essay questions that you should be able to answer when you have completed the chapter and used other study techniques. To help you in reviewing the material, questions have been grouped according to the major sections of the chapter. Of course, you cannot expect your tests to be set up in this way.

▶ AMERICAN COMMUNITIES ◀

Multiple Choice

1. Which one of the following is NOT true of settlement houses?
    a. They were reform communities run by college-educated women.
    b. They were in the midst of the neighborhoods they were trying to help.
    c. They grew from six in 1891 to 400 houses nationwide by 1910.
    d. They were progressives but were often anti-immigrant.

2. Which one of the following was NOT an activity of Lillian Wald's Henry House?
    a. providing health care for immigrants
    b. campaigning for school lunches
    c. working for conservation
    d. encouraging theater, music, and dance

Short Essay

3. Evaluate the effectiveness of the Henry House in helping the residents it served.

▶ THE CURRENTS OF PROGRESSIVISM ◀

Multiple Choice

4. Lillian Wald was to Henry House as THIS person was to Hull House:
    a. Mary Brewster.
    c. Florence Kelley.
    b. Jane Addams.
    d. Rose Schneiderman.

5. Samuel "Golden Rule" Jones and Thomas L. Johnson were examples of city leader/reformers who advocated a change in
    a. policy to improve social welfare for city residents.
    b. the slums and ghetto buildings.
    c. government such as the city commission and manager systems.
    d. voting such as recall and referendum.

6. The "Wisconsin Idea" was promoted by Governor Bob LaFollette as a way of
    a. strengthening direct democracy with direct primaries and other political reforms.
    b. controlling large industries.
    c. protecting state forests and watersheds.
    d. applying academic scholarship and theory to the needs of people.

7. In Jacob Riis's book *How the Other Half Lives,* the "other half" referred to the lives of
    a. women.   c. the urban poor.
    b. African Americans.   d. industrial magnates.

8. *McClure's* was a magazine that published exposés of the nation's social problems. One such series was Lincoln Steffen's study of widespread graft called *The Shame of the*
    a. *Railroads.*   c. *Senate.*
    b. *Cities.*   d. *Oil Companies.*

9. Not only was it a bestseller, but Upton Sinclair's muckraking novel *The Jungle* also resulted in these two federal laws:
    a. the Clayton Anti-Trust Act and the Federal Trade Commission.
    b. the Mann Act and the National Board of Censorship.
    c. the National Municipal Act and Initiative and the Referendum and Recall Act.
    d. the Meat Inspection Act and the Pure Food and Drug Act.

10. Theodore Roosevelt gave them the label "muckrakers." They were
    a. writers who exposed details of social and political evils.
    b. the corrupt political bosses in big city machines.
    c. pessimists who did not accept the progressive idea of reform.
    d. women who wanted more radical things than suffrage reform.

11. The state was to economist Richard Ely as THIS was to philosopher John Dewey:
    a. telic evolution.   c. ethical shift.
    b. education.   d. *Gesellschaft.*

Short Essay

12. How did women such as Jane Addams, Florence Kelley, and Lillian Wald spearhead urban reform?

13. In what ways did the progressive movement draw upon science for guidance?

Extended Essay

14. Use examples to show the three basic attitudes that were common to progressivism.

▶ SOCIAL CONTROL AND ITS LIMITS ◀

Multiple Choice

15. You were MOST likely to be for prohibition if you were
    - a. a working class Catholic.
    - b. a German Lutheran.
    - c. an urban Jew.
    - d. a middle-class Protestant.

16. If you were a teacher trying to follow Elwood Cubberley's ideas, you would be stressing
    - a. vocational manual training programs for a new industrial order.
    - b. educational psychology and guidance counseling.
    - c. assimilation and "Americanization" of immigrant children.
    - d. family education centers to help reform the slums.

Short Essay

17. How was education used to achieve progressive goals?

▶ WORKING-CLASS COMMUNITIES AND PROTEST ◀

Multiple Choice

18. Which one of the following pairs of immigrant settlement and region are INCORRECTLY matched?
    - a. manufacturing towns/New England
    - b. mining camps/West
    - c. turpentine camps/South
    - d. garment trade sweatshops/Pennsylvania and Ohio

19. Which one of the following is NOT a reason that immigrants left southern and eastern Europe to come to America?
    - a. rise in the death rate
    - b. shortage of land
    - c. religious and political persecution
    - d. growth of commercial agriculture

20. Which one of the following immigrants were prevented by law from obtaining American citizenship?
    a. Russian Jews
    b. French Canadians
    c. Japanese
    d. Mexicans

21. The International Ladies Garment Workers Union gained strength and merged working-class women with middle-class reformers as a result of the
    a. Ludlow Massacre.
    b. Triangle Shirtwaist fire.
    c. "Bread and Roses" strike.
    d. "Uprising of the 20,000."

Map Question

22. Which one of the following was NOT one of the top four European countries that was a source of immigrants to the United States between 1900 and 1920?
    a. Germany
    b. Austria-Hungary
    c. Poland
    d. Russia

Short Essay

23. Compare the AFL and the IWW.

24. How did the residents of Greenwich Village combine bohemian sensibility and radical activism?

Extended Essay

25. What role did ethnicity play in the communities and working lives of immigrants?

▶ WOMEN'S MOVEMENTS AND BLACK AWAKENING ◀

Multiple Choice

26. Which one of the following is the RESULT of the other three?
    a. more middle-age women graduate from college
    b. women's clubs emphasize self-help and social reform
    c. more men work in offices
    d. decline in family size

27. Which one of the following authors is NOT correctly matched with his or her work?
    a. Emma Goldman/*Family Limitation*
    b. Booker T. Washington/*Up from Slavery*
    c. Margaret Sanger/*Woman Rebel*
    d. W. E. B. Du Bois/*The Crisis*

28. In terms of racism, southern progressive reformers
    a. advocated complete equality.
    b. thought blacks were incapable of improvement.
    c. were less hostile but still paternalistic.
    d. felt blacks were not part of the New South.

29. Which one of the following has the LEAST association with the other three?
    a. double consciousness   c. talented tenth
    b. Niagara movement   d. *Up from Slavery*

Short Essay

30. Compare the philosophies of Booker T. Washington and W. E. B. Du Bois.

Extended Essay

31. Why was birth control an important element in the liberation of women?

▶ NATIONAL PROGRESSIVISM ◀

Multiple Choice

32. Conservation was to the U.S. Forest Service as THIS was to the National Park Service:
    a. preservation.   c. managed use.
    b. business first.   d. recreation.

33. Which one of the following is NOT a reason that the election of 1912 was the first modern presidential race?
    a. It had the first direct primaries.
    b. There was a great deal of interest group activity.
    c. The candidates avoided issues and "threw mud" instead.
    d. Traditional party loyalties were challenged.

34. Which one of the following did NOT characterize Theodore Roosevelt's progressive philosophy?
   a. The persuasive power of the presidency could be used to guide public opinion.
   b. Wealthy Americans had the right to use their power however they pleased.
   c. Experts could find solutions to national problems.
   d. Centralization was a fact of modern life.

35. Which one of the following issues was the most critical in the development of the West in the twentieth century?
   a. control of railroad monopolies   c. management of water resources
   b. availability of cheap land   d. conservation of wilderness lands

36. Which one of the following was NOT passed during Wilson's first term in office?
   a. Federal Reserve Act   c. Clayton Antitrust Act
   b. Newlands Reclamation Act   d. Underwood-Simmons Act

Map Question

37. In 1912, Wilson became only the second Democrat since the Civil War to be elected to the presidency. He was able to do this because
   a. Eugene Debs drew votes away from the Republicans.
   b. he repeated McKinley's pattern in 1896.
   c. the Republicans split between Taft and Roosevelt.
   d. the state Democratic machines had revived.

Short Essay

38. Why was the Republican Party at such a disadvantage in the presidential election of 1912?

Extended Essay

39. In what ways did Wilson's background make him a natural Progressive Era presidential candidate?

40. Why did some big business figures support federal intrusion into the economy?

Multiple Choice

41. Which one of the following describes the CORRECT order of these events?
    (1) Margaret Sanger begins writing and speaking on birth control.
    (2) Lillian Wald establishes Henry Street Settlement in New York.
    (3) Jane Addams founds Hull House in Chicago.
    (4) Florence Kelley leads National Consumers' League.

    a. 3, 2, 4, 1   c. 2, 3, 4, 1
    b. 4, 2, 3, 1   d. 1, 4, 3, 2

42. The National Association for the Advancement of Colored People (NAACP) was founded in
    a. 1889.   c. 1906.
    b. 1901.   d. 1909.

43. Woodrow Wilson takes the presidency in THIS year, defeating Taft, Roosevelt, and Debs:
    a. 1900.   c. 1908.
    b. 1904.   d. 1912.

44. The Sixteenth Amendment is ratified in THIS year, bringing in a graduated tax:
    a. 1889.   c. 1913.
    b. 1908.   d. 1916.

45. Which one of the following was published in the same year as the Pure Food and Drug Act was passed?
    a. *How the Other Half Lives*   c. *The Jungle*
    b. *The Shame of the Cities*   d. *The Masses*

46. Which one of the following did NOT occur in 1914?
    a. Clayton Antitrust Act passed
    b. National Park Service established
    c. Federal Trade Commission established
    d. Ludlow Massacre

ANSWERS-CHAPTER 21

American Communities
    1. d, pp. 630–631
    2. c, pp. 630–631
    3. p. 631

The Currents of Progressivism
    4. b, p. 633
    5. a, p. 636
    6. d, pp. 636–637
    7. c, p. 638
    8. c, p. 638
    9. d, p. 639
    10. a, p. 639
    11. b, p. 639
    12. p. 634
    13. pp. 634, 639–640
    14. pp. 632–640

Social Control and Its Limits
    15. d, p. 641
    16. c, p. 643
    17. p. 643

Working-Class Communities and Protest
    18. d, p. 643
    19. a, p. 644
    20. c, p. 645
    21. b, p. 646
    22. a, p. 644
    23. pp. 648–649
    24. pp. 649–650
    25. pp. 644–647

Women's Movements and Black
Awakening
    26. b, p. 651
    27. a, pp. 651–653
    28. c, p. 652
    29. d, pp. 652–653
    30. pp. 652–653
    31. p. 651

National Progressivism
    32. a, pp. 655–656
    33. c, p. 658
    34. b, p. 654
    35. c, p. 656
    36. b, pp. 656, 658–659
    37. c, p. 658

    38. pp. 657–658
    39. pp. 657–658
    40. p. 655

Chronology Questions
    41. a, p. 660
    42. d, p. 660
    43. d, p. 660
    44. c, p. 660
    45. c, p. 660
    46. b, p. 660

Name	Position or Title(s)	Major Ideas/ Programs	Actions (Write/Legis./etc.)
Lilian Wald			
Jane Addams			
Florence Kelley			
Robert M. LaFollette			
Clara Lemlich			
William Haywood			
Jacob Riis			
Lincoln Steffens			
Ida Tarbell			
Ray Stannard Baker			
Upton Sinclair			
David Graham Phillips			
Lester Ward			
Edward Ross			
John Dewey			
John R. Commons			

Name	Position or Title(s)	Major Ideas/ Programs	Actions (Write/Legis./etc.)
Richard Ely			
Oliver Wendell Holmes			
Elwood Cubberly			
E. D. Thorndike			
Margaret Sanger			
Booker T. Washington			
W. E. B. Du Bois			
Gifford Pinchot			
John Muir			
Theodore Roosevelt			
Woodrow Wilson			

CHAPTER 22 World War I, 1914-1920

SURVEY

Chapter Overview: This chapter covers the more active foreign policy of the progressive presidents Roosevelt, Taft, and Wilson. America became more interventionist in the western hemisphere, but when war broke out in Europe in 1914, most Americans did not see any national interest at stake. Loyalties were divided, but eventually the United States joined the Allies when Germany broke its pledge on submarine warfare. Americans mobilized rapidly, accepting unprecedented governmental control. A drive to mobilize Americans led to domestic hostility and violations of civil rights. Wilson went to the Peace Conference in Paris with his Fourteen Points to establish a new international ideal, but opponents in Europe and at home and Wilson's own uncompromising attitude defeated his plan. U.S. victory in World War I made it a reluctant world power. In the 1920 election, Americans chose Harding's "normalcy."

Before you begin reading, turn to the CHRONOLOGY at the end of the chapter. Review it to orient yourself in space and time and understand who the leading characters are in the story this chapter will tell. Look for cause and effect relationships. Note unfamiliar terms that you will be learning about. Use the tips and questions at the beginning of Chapter 17 of the Study Guide as a guide for your use of the time line. Return to the CHRONOLOGY after you have read the chapter to see how much you have learned. There is additional information about using the CHRONOLOGY in the Study Skills section of this chapter.

QUESTIONS/READ

As you read each section, use the questions to help you focus on the major themes. Use them as a way to organize note-taking as you read. The objective is for you to be able to answer these questions after you have read the chapter and completed the study skills exercises. Be on the lookout for important terms that you should be able to identify (see the study skills section in Chapter 18 of the Study Guide for tips on how to fully identify these important terms), and do the map exercises as you go along.

AMERICAN COMMUNITIES:
- Explain how vigilante justice in Bisbee, Arizona exemplified the issues and conflicts of American communities during the war.
- **Identify:** Sheriff Wheeler, AFL, IWW, Walter Douglas, Citizens' Protective League, Workers Loyalty League, Senator Red Sutter

BECOMING A WORLD POWER:
- Summarize the ideals and actions of the "progressive diplomacy" of Presidents Theodore Roosevelt, William Howard Taft, and Woodrow Wilson.
- **Identify:** "big stick" policy, Roosevelt Corollary, Panama Canal, Philippe Bunau-Varilla, Open Door, Russo-Japanese War settlement, yellow peril, Root-Takahira Agreement,

"dollar diplomacy," Francisco Madero, Victoriano Huerta, Tampico and Veracruz, ABC Powers, Venustiano Carranza, Pancho Villa, John J. Pershing
- **Map exercise:** *The United States in the Caribbean, 1865–1933* (p. 670) Into what countries did the United States send troops? Which areas were possessions of the United States? What amount of property did American businesses control in Mexico in 1910? What was the involvement of the United States in Guatemala? What countries did the United States financially supervise in this period? What were the canal options and where was it built? Be able to identify the countries and islands shown on this map.

THE GREAT WAR:
- Outline the chain of events through which America entered World War I and the imprint it would leave on America's economy, politics, and cultural life.
- **Identify:** Triple Alliance, Triple Entente, guns of August, Franz Ferdinand, Marne, William Jennings Bryan, National Security League, National Defense Act, *Lusitania* and *Sussex* incidents, Women's Peace Parade, American Union against Militarism, "I Didn't Raise My Boy to Be a Soldier," "He Kept Us Out of War," "Make the world safe for democracy," the Zimmerman Note

AMERICAN MOBILIZATION:
- Discuss the efforts of the American government to mobilize Americans at home and American soldiers overseas.
- Compare and contrast support and opposition to the war among various groups and note any changes of opinion.
- Describe the roles of women and African Americans in the war effort.
- Compare American casualties to those from other countries.
- **Identify:** CPI, George Creel, unhyphenated Americans, Randolph Bourne, Women's Peace Party, Selective Service Act, 369th U.S. Infantry, American Expeditionary Force, Chateau-Thierry, Belleau Wood, Meuse-Argonne
- **Map exercise:** *The Western Front, 1918:* (p. 680) In what country did Americans see the most action in World War I? Know the locations and significance of Cantigny, Belleau Wood, Chateau-Thierry, Second Battle of the Marne, MeuseArgonne, and St. Mihiel. Be able to identify the surrounding countries of Europe.

OVER HERE:
- Summarize the war effort as the ultimate progressive crusade and list the organization trends that would result.
- Describe the impact of the war on business, commercial agriculture, labor, and women.
- **Identify:** War Industries Board, Bernard Baruch, War Service Committees, Herbert Hoover, Food Administration, Liberty Bonds, Radio Corporation of America, Samuel Gompers, National War Labor Board, Immigration Act of 1917, Women In Industry Service, Mary Van Kleeck, Women's Bureau, National Women's Party, Carrie Chapman Catt, Alice Paul, Nineteenth Amendment, Eighteenth Amendment, Raymond Fosdick, Division of Venereal Diseases, Children's Bureau, Julia Lathrop, Maternity and Infancy Act

REPRESSION AND REACTION:
- Explain how participation in World War I increased many existing social tensions in America and what implications this had for the future.

- Describe actions taken by the government and other organizations against radicals and labor unions.
- **Identify:** Espionage and Sedition Acts, Federal Bureau of Investigation, Eugene Debs, *Schenk* v. *United States, Debs* v. *United States, Abrams* v. *United States,* American Protective League, operatives, the Great Migration, East St. Louis and Chicago, James Weldon Johnson, NAACP, Judge Lynch, Governor Coolidge, Elbert Gary
- **Map exercise:** *Woman Suffrage by State, 1869–1919:* (p. 685) Which two states had woman suffrage legislation by 1875? by 1900? by 1915? Where were most of these early suffrage states located? What group of states did not ratify the constitutional amendment? Who was Jeanette Rankin?

AN UNEASY PEACE:
- Describe the struggles of Woodrow Wilson in trying to project his progressive ideas to the world and to his own constituents.
- **Identify:** Big Four, Fourteen Points, Article X, League of Nations, Pan African Congress, war guilt, Treaty of Versailles, Henry Cabot Lodge, irreconcilables, Bolsheviks, Lenin, Brest-Litovsk, Comintern, the Red Scare, A. Mitchell Palmer, red-baiting, 100 percent Americanism, Harding, normalcy

CONCLUSION:
- Summarize the various effects of the war on American life both during and after the war.

REVIEW QUESTIONS: Use these to check your grasp of the major chapter themes. It is good practice to write out essay answers to these questions.

STUDY SKILLS EXERCISES

1. **Vocabulary:**

    vigilante, p. 666   polyglot, p. 677
    consortium, p. 671   armistice, p. 679
    stalemate, p. 673   repression, p. 682
    antagonizing, p. 673   reparations, p. 690
    propaganda, p. 673

2. **Study tip:** If you have been following the study methods suggested, you have already noticed that this text has useful elements for surveying and reviewing: the outline at the beginning of the chapter, the conclusion, and the chronology. The chronology gives you events pertinent to the chapter as well as previous and upcoming events. Look at the Chapter Twenty-two Chronology on page 693. Much may be new to you, but you should at least recognize by surveying the outline and chronology together with the title of the chapter, WORLD WAR I, that your main task is to understand the changes in U.S. foreign policy and the process by which Americans went to war. When you get to the review part of SQ3r, you should use the chronology as a review by answering the questions that are suggested in the Questions/Read section.

    History is a time-organized subject, and even if your professor does not ask dates on a test, you should still pay close attention to dates to give yourself sequence and help yourself comprehend the material. For example, you should note that the *Lusitania* sinking occurs in 1915. It was not the immediate reason that the United States went to war. but the country did begin to lean more to the Allied side. In 1917, you can again see the various steps by which the United States went to war. As you read the chapter, it is easy to lose track of this. You might also look for little tricks called mnemonic devices to help you remember a sequence or list. In this case, the first letters of the main events leading to war are in alphabetical order: L in *Lusitania,* S in Sussex pledge, U in unrestricted submarine warfare resumed, and Z in Zimmerman note—LSUZ. This seems like a silly process, but remembering sequence can help you puzzle out answers on a test even when they are not questions about dates.

3. **Making connections:**
   - Many Latin Americans today still resent American foreign policies and attitudes. Connect the material in Chapter Twenty on empire and the material in this chapter on progressive diplomacy and consider why this resentment developed.
   - Explain the connection between American pursuit of empire, the progressive movement, and the experience of the United States in World War I. (Chapters Twenty and Twenty-one)

4. **Reflections:**
   - Imagine a debate between Jane Addams and George Creel. What would the issues and main points be?
   - If you were in Congress in April 1917, would you have voted yes or no on Wilson's request for a declaration of war? Why would you have voted as you did?
   - How would you have voted in the presidential election of 1920 and why?

RECITE/REVIEW

REVIEW QUESTIONS: This section has a sampling of multiple choice, short essay, and extended essay questions that you should be able to answer when you have completed the chapter and used other study techniques. To help you in reviewing the material, questions have been grouped according to the major sections of the chapter. Of course, you cannot expect your tests to be set up in this way.

▶ AMERICAN COMMUNITIES ◀

Multiple Choice

1. The issue that prompted the vigilante activity in Bisbee, Arizona had to do with
   a. IWW violence.
   b. Palmer's Red Scare tactics.
   c. management-labor conflict.
   d. the Great Migration.

2. Which one of the following did NOT side with or make up part of the vigilante group?
   a. Citizen's Protective League
   b. local authorities and businessmen
   c. Workers Loyalty League
   d. AFL

▶ BECOMING A WORLD POWER ◀

Multiple Choice

3. Which one of the following presidents was NOT a follower of progressive diplomacy?
   a. Theodore Roosevelt
   b. Woodrow Wilson
   c. William Howard Taft
   d. Warren G. Harding

4. President Roosevelt used his "big stick" diplomacy to team up with native forces and foreign promoters like Philippe Bunau-Varilla in order to gain
   a. the Panama Canal zone.
   b. open door advantages in China.
   c. protection for the U.S. Fruit Company in Honduras.
   d. more power in Venezuela against Great Britain, Germany, and Italy.

5. Which one of the following was NOT an area to which Roosevelt and other presidents applied the Monroe Doctrine corollary?
   a. Nicaragua   c. Haiti
   b. Mexico   d. Colombia

6. Which one of the following is the RESULT of the other three?
   a. Wilson withdraws support from Pancho Villa.
   b. Wilson officially recognizes Carranza's government.
   c. Wilson sends U.S. troops to Veracruz, Mexico.
   d. Wilson tries to isolate Huerta from any international support.

Map Questions

7. The United Fruit Company organized the banana trade here in 1899:
   a. Cuba.   c. Honduras.
   b. Nicaragua.   d. Guatemala.

8. Which one of the following was NOT a Caribbean nation that the United States had financial supervision over until 1933?
   a. Costa Rica   c. Haiti
   b. Dominican Republic d. Nicaragua

Short Essay

9. Why was the building of the Panama Canal such an important achievement for the United States?

10. Compare and contrast Roosevelt's and Taft's approach to diplomacy.

▶ THE GREAT WAR ◀

Multiple Choice

11. When the war broke out in Europe, Wilson declared that he would follow this policy toward both sides:
    a. neutrality.   c. dollar diplomacy.
    b. open door.   d. preparedness.

12. Although Wilson's policy meant that the United States could trade with both Germany and England, in practice the United States traded most with England because
    a. of a British naval blockade on all shipping to Germany.
    b. of Germany's policy of surprise submarine attack.
    c. many Americans were biased toward English culture.
    d. the British promised to stay out of Latin America.

13. Which one of the following was NOT one of the events from February of 1917 to March of 1917 that prompted the United States to declare war on Germany?
    a. Germany resumes unrestricted submarine warfare.
    b. The Zimmerman note is discovered and revealed.
    c. Germany sinks seven U.S. merchant ships.
    d. German submarines sink the *Lusitania* and *Sussex*.

14. Which one of the following slogans helped Wilson get re-elected in 1916?
    a. "Keep the World Safe for Democracy."
    b. "He Kept Us Out of War."
    c. "Halt the Hun!"
    d. "Impartial in Thought and Action"

Short Essay

15. Describe the use of propaganda by the European powers during the period leading up to U.S. entry into World War I.

Extended Essay

16. Explain how Wilson's speech asking Congress to declare war in 1917 changed America's role in international affairs.

▶ AMERICAN MOBILIZATION ◀

Multiple Choice

17. Which one of the following has the LEAST in common with the other three?
    a. Randolph Bourne   c. Eugene V. Debs
    b. Jane Addams   d. John Dewey

18. Which one of the following is NOT true of the African American experience in World War I?
   a. Most African Americans were put in the most dangerous combat positions.
   b. French friendliness contrasted with white Americans.
   c. Units were strictly segregated.
   d. African Americans generally supported the war effort.

19. Which one of the following is NOT true about the U. S. Army in World War I?
   a. Of the men who were called up to serve, 12 percent failed to report for duty.
   b. One fifth of the soldiers were born in another country.
   c. Standardized tests showed illiteracy rates of 10 percent.
   d. Immigrants and native-born soldiers were not segregated.

Map Question

20. The majority of action American soldiers saw in World War I was in
   a. Germany.
   b. Russia.
   c. France.
   d. Italy.

Short Essay

21. Describe the use of propaganda by the U.S. government in its attempt to "sell the war."

Extended Essay

22. Compare and contrast the experiences of American armies in World War I and the Civil War, beginning with the draft.

▶ **OVER HERE** ◀

Multiple Choice

23. Which one of the following is NOT correctly matched to the agency led?
   a. WIB/Bernard Baruch converts industrial plants to wartime needs
   b. WIS/Mary Van Kleeck coordinates women's roles in the war effort
   c. NWLB/Eugene Debs leads labor in wartime cooperation
   d. CPI/George Creel promotes the war to the American public

24. Members of the IWW were crucial to which one of the following?
    a. copper mining, lumbering, and wheat harvesting
    b. harvesting alfalfa, cotton, and fruit
    c. work in the building trades, railroads, and coal mines
    d. work in steel mills, truck manufacturing, and shipbuilding

25. Which one of the following was MOST likely to support women's suffrage?
    a. Italian immigrants
    b. German Lutherans
    c. Mormons
    d. Irish mill workers

26. Which one of the following reform issues benefited MOST from anti-German feeling during World War I?
    a. settlement houses
    b. women's suffrage
    c. public health
    d. prohibition

27. Which one of the following was NOT a focus of public health workers during and shortly after World War I?
    a. venereal disease prevention
    b. day care for working mothers
    c. improved prenatal care
    d. research into a cure for influenza

Map Question
28. The first woman elected to Congress was from the state of
    a. Massachusetts.
    b. Montana.
    c. Illinois.
    d. Tennessee.

Short Essay
29. Explain how the war affected different groups in the labor movement, including AFL, Mexican immigrants, and IWW.

Extended Essay
30. How did World War I increase the U.S. government's role in the national economy?

31. Did women's roles in the wartime economy further the cause for women's rights? Defend your answer.

▶ REPRESSION AND REACTION ◀

Multiple Choice

32. The Supreme Court cases of *Schenck* v. *United States, Debs* v. *United States,* and *Abrams* v. *United States,* all upheld
    a. restrictions on union organizing during World War I.
    b. the draft laws of the government during World War I.
    c. extreme wartime restrictions on free speech.
    d. local cases that failed to convict World War I vigilantes.

33. "There is no right to strike against the public safety by anybody, anywhere, any time" was a statement that won this governor national prominence:
    a. Herbert Hoover.
    b. Warren G. Harding.
    c. Calvin Coolidge.
    d. A. Mitchell Palmer.

34. Which one of the following is true?
    a. Few African American men obtained skilled jobs in northern cities.
    b. It was harder for African American women to get jobs than for African American men.
    c. Racial violence was limited to the South.
    d. Local and federal authorities intervened to protect African Americans during urban riots.

Short Essay

35. Describe the role that kinship and community networks played in shaping the Great Migration.

Multiple Choice

36. The "Big Four" was a reference to
    a. the major points of Wilson's wartime peace plan.
    b. American victories at Chateau-Thierry, Belleau Wood, the Meuse Argonne, and Normandy.
    c. four "irreconcilables" who opposed the Versailles Treaty.
    d. the leaders of Britain, France, Italy, and the United States.

37. The most controversial of Wilson's Fourteen Points was his idea of
    a. a League of Nations.
    b. war guilt for Germany.
    c. national self-determination.
    d. free trade.

38. Which one of the following was NOT a group in the Senate that opposed the ratification of the Versailles agreement?
    a. isolationist progressives
    b. Lodge supporters
    c. racists
    d. labor supporters

39. Which one of the following was NOT true about the election of 1920?
    a. The Democratic Party was divided after the fight over the Treaty of Versailles.
    b. The results showed the continued strength of progressivism.
    c. Republicans won on the idea of a return to normalcy.
    d. Americans wanted to stay out of international affairs.

Short Essay

40. What was the Red Scare and what was the legacy it left to the country?

Extended Essay

41. How did U.S. interests fare in the peace negotiations at Versailles?

▶ Chronology Questions ◀

Multiple Choice

42. Which one of the following did NOT occur in 1914?
    a. U.S. forces invaded Mexico.
    b. The Panama Canal opened.
    c. World War I began in Europe.
    d. The Root-Takahira Agreement was accepted.

43. Which one of the following gives these 1917 events in the CORRECT order?
    (1) race riot in East St. Louis, Illinois
    (2) Bolshevik Revolution in Russia
    (3) Zimmerman Note discovered
    (4) Selective Service Act passed

    a. 3, 4, 1, 2
    b. 1, 2, 4, 3
    c. 3, 4, 2, 1
    d. 2, 4, 3, 1

44. The Nineteenth Amendment, on woman suffrage, is ratified in
    a. 1910.
    b. 1915.
    c. 1919.
    d. 1920.

45. A German U-boat sinks the *Lusitania* in
    a. 1914.
    b. 1915.
    c. 1916.
    d. 1917.

46. Which one of the following happened LAST?
    a. Mexican Revolution begins.
    b. Pancho Villa raids New Mexico.
    c. Zimmerman Note suggests a German-Mexican alliance.
    d. U. S. forces invade Mexico.

ANSWERS-CHAPTER 22

American Communities
1. c, p. 666
2. d, pp. 666–667

Becoming A World Power
3. d, p. 668
4. a, p. 668
5. d, p. 669
6. b, pp. 671–672
7. d, p. 670
8. a, p. 670
9. p. 668
10. pp. 668–671

The Great War
11. a, p. 673
12. a, p. 673
13. d, pp. 674–675
14. b, p. 675
15. p. 673
16. p. 675

American Mobilization
17. d, pp. 675–677, 687
18. a, pp. 678, 688
19. c, pp. 677–678
20. c, p. 680
21. p. 676
22. pp. 677–679

Over Here
23. c, pp. 680–683
24. a, p. 682
25. c, p. 684
26. d, p. 685
27. d, p. 686
28. b, p. 685
29. p. 682
30. pp. 680–682
31. pp. 683–684

Repression and Reaction
32. c, p. 687
33. c, p. 689
34. a, p. 688
35. p. 688

An Uneasy Peace
36. d, p. 689
37. a, p. 689
38. d, p. 690
39. b, p. 692
40. p. 692
41. p. 690

Chronology Questions
42. d, p. 693
43. a, p. 693
44. d, p. 693
45. b, p. 693
46. c, p. 693

23 The Twenties, 1920-1929

SURVEY

Chapter Overview: This chapter covers the many changes in American life in the 1920s. After the war, Presidents Harding, Coolidge, and Hoover continued to encourage a foreign policy that would enhance American capitalism. A second industrial revolution based on electrical power, consumer goods, and new management methods took place. The auto age made profound changes in American life and housing patterns. Some areas such as agriculture, railroads, coal mining, and textile manufacturing did not share in the post-war prosperity. A new mass culture defined by radio, movies, music, newspapers, and advertising encouraged a kind of national community. Some groups resisted the changes to modernity and met with mixed results. The postponement of democratic promise continued to stir reaction in women's groups, in Mexican Americans, and in the "New Negro." Intellectuals tried to put into writing the alienation and doubts connected to headlong pursuit of material prosperity.

Before you begin reading, turn to the CHRONOLOGY at the end of the chapter. Review it to orient yourself in space and time and understand who the leading characters are in the story this chapter will tell. Look for cause and effect relationships. Note unfamiliar terms that you will be learning about. Use the tips and questions at the beginning of Chapter 17 of the Study Guide as a guide for your use of the time line. Return to the CHRONOLOGY after you have read the chapter to see how much you have learned.

QUESTIONS/READ

As you read each section, use the questions to help you focus on the major themes. Use them as a way to organize note-taking as you read. The objective is for you to be able to answer these questions after you have read the chapter and completed the study skills exercises. Be on the lookout for important terms that you should be able to identify (see the study skills section in Chapter 18 of the Study Guide for tips on how to fully identify these important terms), and do the map exercises as you go along.

AMERICAN COMMUNITIES: THE MOVIE AUDIENCE AND HOLLYWOOD:
- Explain how Hollywood movies and other vehicles of mass culture created a new national community.
- **Identify:** Roxy, Charlie Chaplin, Mary Pickford, dream factory

POSTWAR PROSPERITY AND ITS PRICE:
- Describe the structural changes in the American economy that developed in the 1920s and the effects those changes had on American life.
- Explain the shift from producer-durable goods to consumer-durable goods.
- Outline the three key areas that brought success to modern corporations.
- Describe the ripple effect of the auto on other industries, the economy in general, and

American society.

- **Identify:** second industrial revolution, Alfred P. Sloan and Owen D. Young, oligopolies, Great Atlantic and Pacific Tea Company, welfare capitalism, American plan, open shop, union shop, closed shop, company unions, William Green, Robert and Helen Lynd, *Middletown,* Empire State Building, Houston, Ida Watkins, Hickman Price, McNary-Haugen Bills, Gastonia, stretch-out

THE NEW MASS CULTURE:

- Describe how the new media of communication reshaped American culture in the 1920s.
- Explain the relationship between advertising and the new communication media.
- Evaluate the significance of sport and celebrity in the 1920s.
- Trace the changes in the treatment of sexuality in the 1920s.
- **Identify:** the studio system, Will Hays, Adolph Zukor, Samuel Goldwyn, William Fox, *The Jazz Singer,* Roscoe "Fatty" Arbuckle, Motion Picture Producers and Distributors Association, KDKA, National Broadcasting System, Columbia Broadcasting System, "The Amos 'n' Andy Show," tabloids, Hearst, Gannett, Scripps-Howard, Walter Winchell, Carter family, Jimmie Rodgers, Bessie Smith, George Herman Ruth, Grantland Rice, William K. Wrigley, Negro National League, Satchel Paige, Red Grange, Jack Dempsey, Gene Tunney, Bill Tilden, Helen Wills, Gertrude Ederle, Johnny Weismuller, the flapper

THE STATE, THE ECONOMY, AND BUSINESS:

- Summarize the continuities of the administrations of Warren Harding, Calvin Coolidge, and Herbert Hoover in domestic and foreign affairs.
- Describe U. S. involvement in foreign affairs and how it connected commerce and foreign policy in the 1920s.
- **Identify:** Ohio gang, Teapot Dome scandal, Andrew Mellon, the "associative state," the Dawes Plan, Charles Evan Hughes, Five Power Treaty, Kellogg-Briand Pact, Pax Americana, Sandino

RESISTANCE TO MODERNITY:

- Summarize the areas of resistance to the major cultural changes of the 1920s.
- Trace the changes in U. S. immigration policy during the 1920s, including the causes for those changes.
- **Identify:** the Volstead Act of 1919, bootlegging, speakeasy, Al Capone, Twenty-first Amendment, "wets" and "drys," Madison Grant, *The Passing of the Great Race,* 1921 Immigration Act, the Johnson-Reed Immigration Act of 1924, new immigrants, American Protective Association, Immigration Restriction League, 100 percent American, Albert Johnson, quota laws, Ku Klux Klan, *The Birth of a Nation,* "Native, White, Protestant Supremacy," religious fundamentalism, the Scopes trial, John Scopes, Clarence Darrow, William Jennings Bryan, H. L. Mencken

PROMISES POSTPONED:

- Outline the efforts of various reform groups, ethnic groups, and intellectuals to redefine their missions, reshape their strategies, and reexamine the material direction of modern American society.
- Explain why the election of 1928 was a referendum on the Republican "new age."
- **Identify:** politicized domesticity, the League of Women Voters, the National Woman's

Party, ERA, 1921 Sheppard–Towner Act, Alice Paul, Mary Anderson, Amelia Earhart, barrios, "greaser," "wetback," *mutualistas,* Federation of Mexican Workers Unions, League of United Latin American Citizens, the "New Negro," Marcus Garvey and his Universal Negro Improvement Association, Langston Hughes, Harlem Renaissance, Claude McKay, Zora Neale Hurston, Jessie Fauset, Countee Collun, James Weldon Johnson, Paul Robeson, Bessie Smith, A. Philip Randolph, lost generation, Ernest Hemingway, *The Sun Also Rises,* F. Scott Fitzgerald, Jazz Age, *The Great Gatsby,* Sinclair Lewis, *Babbitt,* H. L. Mencken, Eugene O'Neill, T. S. Eliot, Ezra Pound, the Fugitives, John Dewey, Walter Lippman, *A Preface to Morals,* Al Smith, "spiritual individualism"

- **Map exercises:** *Black Population, 1920:* (p. 724) What northern cities drew the greatest numbers of African Americans? How many African Americans were there in the North compared to the South? What were the largest southern cities in terms of black population in 1920?
  *Election of 1928: (*p. 728) What states did Democratic candidate Al Smith manage to carry? In what other type of area did he run well? By what margin did Hoover win?

CONCLUSION:
- Describe the status of America in the 1920s.

REVIEW QUESTIONS: Use these to check your grasp of the major chapter themes. It is good practice to write out essay answers to these questions.

STUDY SKILLS EXERCISES

1. Vocabulary:

celluloid, p. 700	normative, p. 712
durables, p. 702	crony, p. 712
synthetic, p. 705	autocratic, p. 716
moguls, p. 706	nativism, p. 718
minstrel, p. 707	alienation, p. 727

2. Making Connections:
- Connect the idea of the "New Negro" to the return of black soldiers from World War I and to Marcus Garvey's philosophy of black pride.
- If your class began with the Reconstruction Period (Chapter 17), what similarities do you see between the aftermath of the Civil War and the Great War?
- Discuss the various connections between mobilization techniques of World War I and the experiences of the decade of the 1920s. (Chapters Twenty-two and Twenty-three)

3. Reflection:
- Imagine yourself attending the opening of the new Roxy Theater or one of the other movie palaces in the 1920s. How do you think you would feel?
- How would you have voted in the 1928 election? What issues would have been important?
- If you could choose one of the new career fields of the 1920s, which one would you choose and why?
- Commentators have argued that the 1920s and the 1980s were similar. Would you agree?

RECITE/REVIEW

REVIEW QUESTIONS: This section has a sampling of multiple choice, short essay, and extended essay questions that you should be able to answer when you have completed the chapter and used other study techniques. To help you in reviewing the material, questions have been grouped according to the major sections of the chapter. Of course, you cannot expect your tests to be set up in this way.

▶ AMERICAN COMMUNITIES ◀

Multiple Choice

1. Which one of the following was not part of the Hollywood "dream factory"?
   a. possibility of material success
   b. a chance to remake one's very identity
   c. the possibility of upward mobility
   d. great social authority

▶ POSTWAR PROSPERITY AND ITS PRICE ◀

Multiple Choice

2. Steam was to the first Industrial Revolution as THIS was to the second one:
   a. coal.
   b. electricity.
   c. oil.
   d. gasoline.

3. The corporate attempt to improve worker well-being and morale in order to challenge the power and appeal of trade unions was known as
   a. the American plan.
   b. associative state.
   c. welfare capitalism.
   d. oligopoly.

4. Cities like Houston, Los Angeles, Miami, and San Diego all shared this in common in the 1920s:
   a. they were automobile suburbs.
   b. they expanded horizontally as their population grew.
   c. the Great Migration of African Americans concentrated there.
   d. textile manufacturers from the New England states moved there.

5. Which one of the following was NOT true of farming in the 1920s?
   a. Farmers in citrus, dairy, and corporate wheatlands thrived.
   b. Tenant farming decreased as agricultural laborers left for the cities.
   c. Net farm income and land values dropped compared to the war years.
   d. American farmers had stiffer competition from overseas agriculture.

6. Which one of the following statements is true of corporations in the 1920s?
   a. Ownership and management were combined.
   b. Corporations focused on a single, core business.
   c. Corporate wealth was concentrated among less than 500 large companies.
   d. Individual entrepreneurs controlled all aspects of a corporation.

Short Essay

7. What is meant by the term "Second Industrial Revolution"?

8. How did the automobile affect American society?

Extended Essay

9. Why did agriculture and older industries miss the country's prosperity and progress during the 1920s?

▶ THE NEW MASS CULTURE ◀

Multiple Choice

10. Warner Brother made a huge hit by bringing out the first "talkie," which was
    a. *The Birth of a Nation.*
    c. *The Jazz Singer.*
    b. *The Love of Sunya.*
    d. *Amos and Andy.*

11. Walter Winchell typified the 1920s new popularity of
    a. tabloid gossip.
    c. Hollywood stars.
    b. radio announcers.
    d. sports writers.

12. Advertising of the 1920s paid most attention to THIS aspect:
    a. price of the product.
    c. quality of product.
    b. U.S.A. made.
    d. needs of consumer.

13. Gene Tunney, Gertrude Ederle, Satchel Paige, and Bill Tilden all illustrate the new celebrity of
    a. sports heroes.
    c. sports writers.
    b. radio announcers.
    d. radio stars.

14. Which one of the following from the United States had the GREATEST impact on Canada and Mexico?
    a. movies
    c. radio
    b. newspapers
    d. baseball

Short Essay

15. How did Hollywood "censor itself" in the face of calls for government censorship of the film-making industry?

16. How did "Babe" Ruth repair baseball's image after the "Black Sox" scandal?

Extended Essay

17. In what ways did sex and sensuality take a more obvious role in the culture of the 1920s?

▶ THE STATE, THE ECONOMY, AND BUSINESS ◀

Multiple Choice

18. The Teapot Dome scandal involved questionable federal involvement on the part of Interior Secretary Albert Fall in leasing
    a. national forests to lumber companies.
    b. navy oil reserves to oil developers.
    c. federal facilities and vehicles to Prohibition violators.
    d. buildings and supplies for the Veterans Bureau.

19. As Secretary of Commerce in the Coolidge Administration, Herbert Hoover worked with Chicago banker Dawes on a plan to aid the recovery of
    a. tenant farmers.   c. the German economy.
    b. revolutionary China.   d. Central American countries.

20. Andrew Mellon is associated with
    a. receiving bribes from violators of prohibition.
    b. tax cuts for the wealthy.
    c. post-World War I arms reduction.
    d. increasing American investment abroad.

21. Aggressive United States investment in Latin America resulted in all the following EXCEPT
    a. the difficulty for Latin Americans in growing their own foods.
    b. the U.S. takeover of mineral resources.
    c. the inability to diversify the Latin American economy.
    d. the growth of democratic governments.

Short Essay

22. Describe the connection between foreign policy and commerce in the United States after World War I.

Extended Essay

23. How did Herbert Hoover reflect Calvin Coolidge's attitude about the relationship between government and business?

▶ RESISTANCE TO MODERNITY ◀

Multiple Choice

24. Although consumption of alcohol per capital did decrease overall during Prohibition, it increased in this group:
    a. Bohemian radicals.
    b. working-class immigrants.
    c. Lost Generation writers.
    d. youth and college students.

25. The "new immigrants" from 1890 to 1920 referred to
    a. African Americans migrating from the South to the North.
    b. Mexican laborers, both legal and illegal.
    c. Southern and Eastern Europeans.
    d. Asians from the Philippines and Japan.

26. Which one of the following was NOT a group to which the revived Ku Klux Klan expanded its hostility?
    a. Protestants
    b. Jews
    c. Catholics
    d. Darwinists

27. Which one of the following had the LEAST to do with the other three?
   a. John Scopes
   b. Clarence Darrow
   c. William Jennings Bryan
   d. H. L. Mencken

Short Essay

28. Describe the changes in U. S. immigration policy between 1920 and 1924.

Extended Essay

29. In what ways was science misused to support the dominant racist theories of the time?

▶ PROMISES POSTPONED ◀

Multiple Choice

30. Which one of the following would have been the LEAST likely to promote the idea of politicized domesticity?
   a. League of Women Voters
   b. National Women's Party
   c. Women's Trade Union League
   d. National Consumers League

31. Writers Langston Hughes, Zora Neale Hurston, James Weldon Johnson, and others belonged to a 1920s group called the
   a. Lost Generation of expatriate writers.
   b. Fugitives from the South.
   c. New Negro of the Harlem Renaissance.
   d. Ohio gang.

32. Which one of the following groups would have been the LEAST likely to vote for Al Smith in the 1928 election?
   a. American Protective Association
   b. a group against prohibition
   c. Brotherhood of Sleeping Car Porters
   d. newer immigrant groups

33. Which one of the following statements is NOT true of Mexicans in the 1920s?
    a. They were included in the immigration laws of 1921 and 1924.
    b. Mexican immigration doubled in the 1920s compared to the previous decade.
    c. Mexicans worked in sugar beet fields in Michigan.
    d. Mexican immigrants in the 1920s were likely to remain permanent residents of the United States.

34. Which one of the following authors is NOT correctly matched with his work?
    a. Ernest Hemingway/*A Farewell to Arms*
    b. F. Scott Fitzgerald/*The Waste Land*
    c. Sinclair Lewis/*Babbitt*
    d. Eugene O'Neill/*The Emperor Jones*

35. Which one of the following would be LEAST likely to support Sacco and Vanzetti?
    a. H. L. Mencken
    b. Felix Frankfurter
    c. Edmund Wilson
    d. John Dewey

Map Questions

36. Which one of the following was NOT among the southern cities having the highest African American population in 1920?
    a. New Orleans
    c. Miami
    b. Birmingham
    d. Atlanta

37. Which one of the following cities was closest to an area that had a black population greater than 10 percent?
    a. New York
    c. Chicago
    b. St. Louis
    d. Philadelphia

38. The only areas that were a strong showing for Al Smith in the 1928 presidential election were in the
    a. largest cities and the Deep South.
    b. Midwest and Great Plains.
    c. Pacific coast and Northwest.
    d. rural areas of the West.

Short Essay

39. What was the Harlem Renaissance?

40. What were the two main wings of the women's movement in the 1920s and what were the goals of each?

Extended Essay

41. Use specific examples to describe the main concerns of both black and white intellectuals in the 1920s.

42. Were the twenties really "roaring" for all Americans? Defend your answer with specific examples.

▶ CHRONOLOGY QUESTIONS ◀

Multiple Choice

43. The Equal Rights Amendment was first introduced to Congress in
    a. 1920.   c. 1926.
    b. 1923.   d. 1928.

44. Robert and Helen Lynd publish their classic community study *Middletown* in
    a. 1923.   c. 1927.
    b. 1925.   d. 1929.

45. Which one of the following does NOT happen in 1927?
    a. The Scopes trial proceeds.   c. Lindbergh flies solo across the Atlantic.
    b. *The Jazz Singer* is shown.   d. The McNary-Haugen Farm bill was vetoed.

46. Which one of the following lists the correct chronological order of events?
    (1) Five-Power Treaty   (3) Calvin Coolidge becomes president
    (2) Kellog-Briand Pact   (4) Dawes Plan

    a. 3, 1, 4, 2   c. 3, 4, 2, 1
    b. 1, 3, 4, 2   d. 4, 3, 2, 1

ANSWERS-CHAPTER 23

American Communities
1. d, pp. 697–698

Postwar Prosperity and Its Price
2. b, p. 699
3. c, p. 701
4. b, p. 704
5. b, p. 704
6. c, p. 700
7. p. 699
8. pp. 702–703
9. pp. 704–705

The New Mass Culture
10. c, p. 706
11. a, p. 708
12. d, p. 709
13. a, p. 711
14. c, pp. 707–708
15. p. 707
16. p. 710
17. p. 712

The State, The Economy, and Business
18. b, p. 713
19. c, p. 714
20. b, p. 713
21. d, pp. 715–716
22. pp. 715–716
23. pp. 713–714

Resistance to Modernity
24. d, p. 716
25. c, pp. 716–717
26. a, pp. 718–719
27. c, p. 720
28. pp. 716–718
29. p. 717

Promises Postponed
30. b, p. 721
31. c, p. 725
32. a, p. 728
33. a, p. 722
34. b, p. 726
35. d, pp. 726–727
36. c, p. 724
37. d, p. 724
38. a, p. 728

39. pp. 724–725
40. p. 721
41. pp. 725–727
42. pp. 704–706, 720–729

Chronology Questions
43. b, p. 729
44. d, p. 729
45. a, p. 729
46. b, p. 729

CHAPTER 24

The Great Depression and the New Deal, 1929-1940

SURVEY

Chapter Overview: This chapter covers the cumulative effect of underlying weaknesses of the economy and the stock market crash that led to the Depression. Many unemployed workers blamed themselves rather than the system, but more began to look to the government for some relief. President Hoover's response was consistent with his stated views, but many began to demand more action and elected Democratic reformer Franklin Delano Roosevelt. His first New Deal was a cooperative business-government venture, but in his second, he made a more dramatic shift, although not to the radicalism some critics accused him of. Other critics said he was not radical enough. Roosevelt's own ability to inspire, the activism of his wife, and the action-oriented programs regained American confidence even though this did not end the Depression. FDR's impatience with the Supreme Court and his attempt to pack it cost him some political influence. Deep poverty was not really touched by the programs and minorities did not make major gains, but they did form a coalition of voters that supported the Democratic Party.

Before you begin reading, turn to the CHRONOLOGY at the end of the chapter. Review it to orient yourself in space and time and understand who the leading characters are in the story this chapter will tell. Look for cause and effect relationships. Note unfamiliar terms that you will be learning about. Use the tips and questions at the beginning of Chapter 17 of the Study Guide as a guide for your use of the time line. Return to the CHRONOLOGY after you have read the chapter to see how much you have learned.

QUESTIONS/READ

As you read each section, use the questions to help you focus on the major themes. Use them as a way to organize note-taking as you read. The objective is for you to be able to answer these questions after you have read the chapter and completed the study skills exercises. Be on the lookout for important terms that you should be able to identify (see the study skills section in Chapter 18 of the Study Guide for tips on how to fully identify these important terms), and do the map exercises as you go along.

AMERICAN COMMUNITIES: SIT-DOWN STRIKE AT FLINT:
* Describe the power of community as exemplified by the Flint sit-down strike in 1936.
* Evaluate the significance of this strike.
* **Identify:** Federal Emergency Relief Administration, Works Progress Administration, Wagner Act, Women's Emergency Brigade, Battle of Running Bulls

HARD TIMES:
* Summarize the reasons why the Great Depression occurred.
* Trace the growth of unemployment and describe its financial, psychological, and social consequences.

- Describe how the Hoover administration responded to the Depression.
- **Identify:** bull market, "buying on the margin," Black Tuesday, Wall Street Crash of 1929, Andrew Mellon, President's Emergency Committee for Unemployment, Organization for Unemployment Relief, Reconstruction Finance Corporation, Emergency Relief Act, Farmers' Holiday Association, Bonus Army, Douglas MacArthur
- **Map exercise:** *The Election of 1932:* (p. 741) Which states did Hoover manage to carry in 1932? How did FDR's popular vote compare to Hoover's in 1928?

FDR AND THE FIRST NEW DEAL:
- Compare the government responses under Hoover and Roosevelt to the problems of mass unemployment and other effects of the Great Depression. Follow this theme throughout the chapter.
- Describe the connection between FDR's personality and the success of the first New Deal.
- **Identify:** Eleanor Roosevelt, Temporary Emergency Relief Administration, brain trust, bank holiday, fireside chat, Emergency Banking Act, the Hundred Days, Civilian Conservation Corps (CCC), Federal Emergency Relief Administration (FERA), Harry Hopkins, Agricultural Adjustment Administration (AAA), parity prices, subsidy, Southern Tenant Farmers Union (STFU), Tennessee Valley Authority (TVA), National Industrial Recovery Act (NIRA), National Recovery Administration (NRA), "priming the pump," Public Works Administration (PWA)

LEFT TURN AND THE SECOND NEW DEAL:
- Outline the views of critics, both right and left, of Roosevelt's New Deal programs and describe Roosevelt's response.
- Describe how the New Deal affected the upsurge of labor.
- Describe the significant issues and the outcome of the 1936 election.
- **Identify:** Father Coughlin, Al Smith, Upton Sinclair, Francis E. Townsend, Huey Long, "Every Man a King," Section 7a of NIRA, American Liberty League, Second Hundred Days, Emergency Relief Appropriation Act, Works Progress Administration, Social Security Act, National Labor Relations Act, "the Magna Carta for Labor," Resettlement Administration (RA), John Maynard Keynes, Rexford G. Tugwell, Greenhills and Greendale, CIO, John L. Lewis, Sidney Hillman, Frances Perkins, Memorial Day Massacre, the New Deal Coalition, Alf Landon

THE NEW DEAL AND THE WEST:
- Describe the immediate and long-range effect of New Deal measures in the West.
- Trace the changes in land use patterns and conservation practices in the Dust Bowl from the 1920s through World War II.
- **Identify:** Dust Bowl, "Okies," Drought Relief Service, Taylor Grazing Act of 1934, Soil Conservation Service, Bureau of Reclamation, Boulder (Hoover) Dam, All-American Canal, Central Valley Project, Grand Coulee Dam, John Collier, BIA, Indian Reorganization Act (IRA) of 1934, the Margold opinion
- **Map exercises:** *The Dust Bowl, 1935–1940:* (p. 749) What states were affected by the Dust Bowl? Where was it most severe? What federal programs were there and what effect did they have on migration?
The New Deal and Water: (p. 752) What states were affected by the Tennessee Valley

Authority? What river was harnessed? Identify the various dams and canals associated with different western water projects.

DEPRESSION-ERA CULTURE:
- Discuss how American popular culture was shaped during the Depression.
- Describe the impact of Communism in America in the 1930s.
- **Identify:** Federal Project No. 1, Lewis Hine, Federal Writers Project, Life in America Series, Hallie Flanagan, "Living Newspaper," *Index of American Design,* the documentary impulse, Roy Stryker, John Steinbeck's *The Grapes of Wrath,* Ma Joad, Margaret Mitchell's *Gone with the Wind,* Scarlett O'Hara, Sherwood Anderson's *Puzzled America* and James Rorty's *Where Life Is Better,* pitiless publicity, "Waiting for Lefty," the American Communist Party, Marxist analysis, the "Popular Front," the Abraham Lincoln Brigade, Walt Disney, Frank Capra, the Golden Age of Radio, "swing," Benny Goodman, Duke Ellington, Fletcher Henderson

THE LIMITS OF REFORM:
- Summarize the legacy of the New Deal for various areas and people of America.
- Compare the first programs of Roosevelt to the second reform package and the changes that were labeled the "Roosevelt recession."
- Evaluate the effectiveness of the New Deal in ending the Depression. (Draw from the whole chapter in answering this question.)
- **Identify:** court packing, *Schecter* v. *United States, Butler* v. *United States,* the women's network, Eleanor Roosevelt, *It's Up to the Women,* Ellen Woodward, Molly Dewson, Frances Perkins, Clifford Burke, the "Black Cabinet"

CONCLUSION:
- Summarize the legacies of the Great Depression and of the New Deal.

STUDY SKILLS EXERCISES

1. **Vocabulary:**

economic crisis, p. 733	zeal, p. 753
bull market, p. 735	fomenting, p. 756
hoarding, p. 742	stereotyping, p. 761
scab workers, p. 747	

2. Make a chart of all the New Deal programs with their directors, their nature, and their impact (constitutional questions or rulings, if any). See the sample on page 279 at the end of this chapter of the Study Guide.

3. **Making connections:**
   - What practices were being established at the turn of the century in farming (Chapter 18) that affected the development of the Dust Bowl? What practices established in the New Deal in farming and water policy still affect us now?
   - What programs proposed by the populists (Chapter 20) were enacted in the New Deal?
   - Compare the Dawes Act provisions from Chapter Eighteen to the Indian Reorganization Act in this chapter.

4. Reflections:
- How would you have voted in 1932, 1934, 1936, and 1938 and why?
- Imagine yourself one of Roosevelt's "Brain Trust" people. What would you advise?
- Imagine yourself as a Roosevelt critic. What would your points be?

RECITE/REVIEW

REVIEW QUESTIONS: This section has a sampling of multiple choice, short essay, and extended essay questions that you should be able to answer when you have completed the chapter and used other study techniques. To help you in reviewing the material, questions have been grouped according to the major sections of the chapter. Of course, you cannot expect your tests to be set up in this way.

▶ AMERICAN COMMUNITIES ◀

Multiple Choice

1. The "Battle of the Running Bulls" referred to
   a. the sporting arena atmosphere of the bull market in the 1920s.
   b. the government's ownership of the cattle industry.
   c. labor strife at General Motors in Flint.
   d. Roosevelt's conflict with conservative Supreme Court justices.

▶ HARD TIMES ◀

Multiple Choice

2. Which one of the following statements is NOT true?
   a. In the 1920s, paper value of stocks outran their real value.
   b. Buying on margin brought new buyers into the stock market.
   c. Corporations put most of their profits into developing new technologies.
   d. About one in thirty Americans owned stocks in the 1920s.

3. Which one of the following was the greatest weakness in the 1920s economy?
   a. too many Americans were invested in the stock market
   b. unequal distribution of wealth
   c. consumers saved rather than spent their discretionary income
   d. increasing mechanization encouraged overproduction by farmers

4. Which one of the following statements is true?
   a. Unemployment during the Depression never surpassed 20 percent.
   b. Unemployment in 1939 was below 10 percent.
   c. The unemployment crisis ended with Roosevelt's election.
   d. Unemployment reached its peak in 1933.

5. Which one of the following was NOT characteristic of the unemployment situation during the Depression?
   a. Many workers blamed themselves for being unemployed.
   b. There was no unemployment insurance.
   c. Women found it harder to get work than men did.
   d. Unemployment changed the nature of family relationships.

6. Communist organizers were associated with
    a. the Iowa farm holiday.
    b. the Detroit auto workers demonstration.
    c. the Bonus Army.
    d. local relief efforts for the unemployed.

Map Question

7. Hoover's only strength in the 1932 election was in
    a. the West.
    b. the South.
    c. New England.
    d. the Midwest.

Short Essay

8. What was the relationship of the stock market crash to the causes of the Great Depression?

9. What was the goal of Hoover's Reconstruction Finance Corporation (RFC)?

Extended Essay

10. How did Hoover's political philosophy and experience influence his responses to the Depression?

▶FDR AND THE FIRST NEW DEAL◀

Multiple Choice

11. When FDR became president, one of the first things he did to re-establish confidence in the economy was
    a. set up the Temporary Emergency Relief Administration.
    b. declare a four-day bank holiday to shore up the banking system.
    c. establish the President's Emergency Committee for Unemployment.
    d. have Congress create the Reconstruction Finance Corporation.

12. The Agricultural Adjustment Administration was set up on principles based on proposals made by this earlier group:
    a. 1900s progressives.
    c. 1890s Populists.
    b. Patrons of Husbandry.
    d. American Socialist Party.

13. The Public Works Administration, or PWA, was based on the principle of "priming the pump," which meant stimulating the economy through
    a. providing jobs and increasing consumer spending.
    b. making credit available to businesses, banks, and industries.
    c. encouraging small businesses and self-employment.
    d. setting prices at 1909–1914 purchasing power average.

Short Essay

14. How did FDR attempt to restore economic confidence in the United States?

▶ LEFT TURN AND THE SECOND NEW DEAL ◀

Multiple Choice

15. Al Smith was to the American Liberty League as Huey Long was to the
    a. American Socialist Party.
    b. Abraham Lincoln Brigade.
    c. EPIC Society.
    d. Share Our Wealth Society.

16. When militant union leaders John L. Lewis and Sidney Hillman pushed to form a committee within the AFL to study industrial organizing, their goal was to
    a. run their own presidential candidate for the 1936 election.
    b. set up unions of mass production workers by industry rather than by craft.
    c. draw all unions together into one huge and powerful organization.
    d. persuade Roosevelt to enact more social reform programs.

17. This Kansas Republican and editor of the Emporia Gazette attacked the New Deal for building up the Federal Government and creating a "Great Political Machine" centered in Washington:
    a. Alfred Landon.
    b. Al Smith.
    c. William Allen White.
    d. Frances Perkins.

18. Which one of the following traditionally Republican groups went Democratic in the election of 1936?
    a. trade unionists
    b. African Americans
    c. farmers
    d. ethnic workers in large cities

Short Essay

19. How did the New Deal support the growth of organized labor?

Extended Essay

20. How did FDR's political opponents influence him during the "Second Hundred Days"?

21. Were FDR's New Deal activities socialistic as many of his critics claimed?

▶ THE NEW DEAL AND THE WEST ◀

Multiple Choice

22. Which one of the following was the RESULT of the other three?
    a. growth in mechanized farming on the Great Plains
    b. federal government purchase of 8 million head of cattle
    c. severe soil erosion on the Great Plains
    d. falling wheat prices

23. If you were a western voter in 1932, Roosevelt's support for this was significant in winning your political backing:
    a. Boulder Dam.   c. TVA.
    b. All-American Canal.   d. Central Valley Project.

24. Overall, federal agricultural and reclamation programs probably helped this group the most:
    a. sharecroppers.   c. large-scale farmers.
    b. Indians living on reservations.   d. farm workers.

25. Under John Collier and the Indian Reorganization Act, the Bureau of Indian Affairs did much to improve Indian situations. The heart of the IRA and Collier's attitude was
    a. strengthening the assimilation programs of the Dawes Act.
    b. the Committee of Indian Reorganization (CIO) to lobby the Congress.
    c. preserving Indian history through the Federal Writers Project.
    d. to restore tribal structures and tribal power to Indian groups.

Map Question

26. Which one of the following states did not experience the most severe wind erosion during the years 1935–1938?
    a. Nebraska   c. Oklahoma
    b. Kansas   d. Colorado

27. Boulder Dam is to the Colorado River Project as _____ is to the Columbia River Project.
    a. Hoover Dam
    b. California Aqueduct
    c. Grand Coulee Dam
    d. All-American Canal

Short Essay

28. What was the impact on western life of the New Deal's water projects?

Extended Essay

29. Evaluate the work of John Collier as head of the Bureau of Indian Affairs.

▶ DEPRESSION-ERA CULTURE ◀

Multiple Choice

30. The "Living Newspaper" was
    a. part of the Federal Theater Project.
    b. a documentary film.
    c. a weekly radio news program.
    d. an inexpensive tabloid.

31. What percentage of Americans attended a movie weekly during the Depression?
    a. 20 percent
    b. 45 percent
    c. 60 percent
    d. 75 percent

32. Which one of the following artists is incorrectly matched with his or her art?
    a. Dorothea Lange/documentary photographer
    b. John Steinbeck/novelist
    c. Clifford Odetts/playwright
    d. Walker Evans/painter

33. FDR's fireside chats and Charles Coughlin's National Union for Social Justice shared what in common?
    a. more leftist ideas
    b. potential power of radio
    c. wanting more federal activism
    d. populist/progressive mixtures

34. The Federal Communications Commission's main impact was from
    a. establishing a program to investigate Communist influence in Hollywood.
    b. censorship of radio programs.
    c. its policies that favored commercial broadcasting.
    d. support for unemployed writers.

Short Essay

35. What was the "documentary impulse" of 1930s America?

36. Why did Marxist analysis become prominent during the 1930s?

Extended Essay

37. Using specific examples, describe some of the contradictory messages that were reflected in the culture of the Depression.

Multiple Choice

38. *Schecter* v. *United States* was to the National Recovery Administration as *Butler* v. *United States* was to the
    a. National Labor Relations Act.
    b. Reclamation Bureau.
    c. Federal Theater Project.
    d. Agricultural Adjustment Administration.

39. Which one of the following is the CAUSE of the others?
    a. Federal Reserve System tightens credit policies.
    b. Federal spending is cut back—especially in the WPA and farm programs.
    c. The Roosevelt recession worsens economic conditions.
    d. The Fair Labor Standards Act is passed.

40. While New Deal programs were less numerous by 1938, the Fair Labor Standards Act established this first:
    a. federal minimum wage.
    b. credit card laws.
    c. public housing construction.
    d. closed shop.

Short Essay

41. Why was FDR fearful of taking on the plight of black people during the Depression?

Extended Essay

42. Why, in retrospect, were FDR's attacks on Hoover during the 1932 presidential campaign somewhat ironic?

Multiple Choice

43. Which one of the following lists the correct chronological order of events?
    (1) FDR is elected president for first time.
    (2) A sit-down strike begins at the General Motors Plant in Flint, Michigan.
    (3) The Twenty-first Amendment repeals prohibition.
    (4) The Bonus Army marches on Washington, D. C.

    a. 1, 4, 2, 3   c. 4, 1, 3, 2
    b. 2, 3, 1, 4   d. 3, 4, 2, 1

44. Which one of the following does NOT happen in 1935?
    a. The Committee for Industrial Organization is established.
    b. The Second New Deal begins.
    c. Dust storms turn the southern Great Plains into the Dust Bowl.
    d. The Dawes Severalty Act is repealed.

45. This Act, which established the first federal minimum wage, was enacted in 1938:
    a. National Housing Act.   c. Fair Labor Standards Act.
    b. Wagner-Steagall Act.   d. the New Deal.

46. Which one of the following occurred in 1937?
    a. sit-down strike at General Motors plant in Flint, Michigan
    b. General Motors recognizes United Auto Workers
    c. Congress of Industrial Unions formed
    d. Fair Labor Standards Act passed

ANSWERS-CHAPTER 24

American Communities
    1. c, p. 716

Hard Times
    2. c, p. 735
    3. b, p. 737
    4. d, p. 738
    5. c, pp. 737–739
    6. b, p. 740
    7. c, p. 741
    8. pp. 735–737
    9. p. 740
    10. pp. 739–740

FDR and the First New Deal
    11. b, p. 741
    12. c, p. 743
    13. a, p. 744
    14. pp. 741–742

Left Turn and the Second New Deal
    15. d, p. 745
    16. b, p. 747
    17. c, p. 748
    18. b, p. 748
    19. pp. 746–747
    20. pp. 744–746
    21. p. 748

The New Deal and The West
    22. b, pp. 749–750
    23. a, p. 751
    24. c, p. 751
    25. d, pp. 753–754
    26. a, p. 749
    27. c, p. 752
    28. pp. 751–753
    29. pp. 753–754

Depression-Era Culture
    30. a, p. 755
    31. c, p. 757
    32. d, pp. 756–757
    33. b, pp. 745, 759
    34. c, p. 759
    35. pp. 754, 756–757
    36. p. 757
    37. pp. 754–759

The Limits of Reform/Conclusion
    38. d, p. 761
    39. b, p. 764
    40. a, p. 764
    41. p. 763
    42. pp. 740, 764

Chronology Questions
    43. c, p. 765
    44. d, p. 765
    45. c, p. 765
    46. b, p. 765

CHAPTER 24 – STUDY SKILLS EXERCISE #1

SIGNIFICANT LEGISLATION DURING THE 1932 AND 1936 ROOSEVELT ADMINISTRATIONS

Name of the Program	Date	Director	Nature of the Program	Impact of the Program
Banking Holiday				
Emergency Banking Act				
Civilian Conservation Corps (CCC)				
Federal Emergency Relief Admin. (FERA)				
Agricultural Adjust. Act (AAA)				
Tennessee Valley Auth. (TVA)				
National Industrial Recovery Act (NIRA)				
a. NRA				
b. PWA				
Indian Reorganization Act (IRA)				
Resettlement Admin. (RA)				
Works Progress Admin. (WPA)				
National Labor Relations Act (NLRA)				
Social Security Act				
Soil Conserv. Districts				
Nat. Housing Act (1934–1937)				
Fair Labor Standards Act				

CHAPTER 25

World War II, 1941–1945

SURVEY

Chapter Overview: This chapter covers the American involvement in World War II and its effects on the United States. America began trying to ensure isolation by enacting a series of neutrality laws, but as the war broke out in Europe and Asia, the United States gradually altered the neutrality laws. Even before Pearl Harbor, the United States was involved in conflict with Germany in the North Atlantic. U. S. policy was to deal with Hitler first, but the Japanese attack on Pearl Harbor changed that. The United States and its allies were on the defensive until mid-1942, when the North Africa offensive and the Coral Sea-Midway victories slowly turned the tide. The war became a battle of production with the U. S. possessing the advantages. While the United States fought the war for democracy, some constituencies still had to fight for democracy at home. The home front involvement in the war changed the lives of many women, African Americans, and Japanese Americans. As victory was in sight, the United States was the major world power and at the center of global politics. Leaders tried to develop a new foreign policy to face these changing conditions.

Before you begin reading, turn to the CHRONOLOGY at the end of the chapter. Review it to orient yourself in space and time and understand who the leading characters are in the story this chapter will tell. Look for cause and effect relationships. Note unfamiliar terms that you will be learning about. Use the tips and questions at the beginning of Chapter 17 of the Study Guide as a guide for your use of the time line. Return to the CHRONOLOGY after you have read the chapter to see how much you have learned.

QUESTIONS/READ

As you read each section, use the questions to help you focus on the major themes. Use them as a way to organize note-taking as you read. The objective is for you to be able to answer these questions after you have read the chapter and completed the study skills exercises. Be on the lookout for important terms that you should be able to identify (see the study skills section in Chapter 18 of the Study Guide for tips on how to fully identify these important terms), and do the map exercises as you go along.

AMERICAN COMMUNITIES:
- Using the Los Alamos scientists as your example, discuss the problems in American communities created by wartime changes
- **Identify:** Manhattan project, Enrico Fermi, Robert Oppenheimer, "the gadget"

THE COMING OF WORLD WAR II:
- Trace the changes in American policy from isolationism to involvement in the war in Europe and Asia, and also trace the changes in reactionary critics to the policy.
- Describe the events that foreshadowed the possible outbreak of war in Europe and the Pacific.

- Outline the beginning of the war and the response of the United States in Europe and the Pacific.
- **Identify:** Fascists, Mussolini, *Lebensraum,* Rome-Berlin Axis, Munich Conference, *Kristallnacht,* Nye Committee, *All Quiet on the Western Front,* Neutrality Acts, Norman Thomas, Keep America Out of War Congress, American League Against War and Fascism, America First Committee, Robert Taft, "quarantine the aggressors," Nazi-Soviet Pact, *Blitzkrieg,* Neutrality Act of 1939, Selective Service Act of 1940, Lend-Lease, security zone and defensive waters, Atlantic Charter, Pearl Harbor, Jeannette Rankin

ARSENAL OF DEMOCRACY:
- Describe how Roosevelt set about making the United States an arsenal of democracy.
- Compare the size and focus of federal government efforts under the War Powers Act and the New Deal.
- Outline the Allied advantages that allowed them to win the war.
- Describe how the war affected workers and the labor movement.
- **Identify:** the War Powers Act, Supply Priorities and Allocation Board, Office of Price Administration, Office of War Information, Federal Bureau of Investigation, Office of Strategic Services, the War Production Board, Food for Freedom, *bracero* program, "Rosie the Riveter," National War Labor Board, "hate strikes," wildcat strikes, John L. Lewis, federal anti-strike laws

THE HOME FRONT:
- Summarize the effects of the war on the home front, including business, labor, the family, and various ethnic groups.
- **Identify:** "Share Your Home," latch-key children, John L. DeWitt, Issei, Executive Order 9066, internment camps, Japanese American Citizens League, *Korematsu* v. *United States,* Tule Lake, the "Double V" campaign, A. Philip Randolph, Pauli Murray, Executive Order 8802, CORE, NAACP, Zoot-Suit Riots, Office of Inter-American Affairs, International Sweethearts of Rhythm, "good war," Captain America, "Loose Lips Sink Ships"

MEN AND WOMEN IN UNIFORM:
- Describe the effects the war had on men and women in uniform.
- Identify: Generals MacArthur and Eisenhower, George Marshall, GI, battle fatigue, Eddie Slovik, Stimson, "sociological laboratory," 99th Pursuit Squadron, Charles Drew, *Nisei,* 442nd, *Twenty-Seven Soldiers,* the Bataan Death March
- **Map exercise:** *Wartime Army Camps, Naval Bases, and Airfields:* (p. 787) Where were most military facilities concentrated? What new areas were opened up?

THE WORLD AT WAR:
- Outline the strategies needed to win the war in both Europe and the Pacific.
- Identify the significant turning points of the war.
- **Identify:** Moscow, Stalingrad, Kursk, El Alamein, Operation Torch, Casablanca, B-17, Dresden, Sicily, Warsaw Ghetto, partisans, Operation Overlord, D-Day, Charles de Gaulle, the Battle of the Bulge, Arnhem, Ruhr, "island hopping," Stillwell, Coral Sea, Operation Magic, MacArthur, Nimitz, Tarawa, Leyte Gulf, Okinawa, *kamikaze*

- **Map exercises:** *War in Europe:* (p. 793) Who were the Axis powers and what did they control at their height? Be able to locate Stalingrad, El Alamein, Sicily, Normandy, and the Battle of the Bulge.

  War in the Pacific: (p. 797) What was the extent of Japanese control by August of 1942? As you look at this map, why do you think "island hopping" was a wise strategy? Be able to locate Pearl Harbor, the Coral Sea, Midway, Leyte Gulf, Okinawa, Hiroshima, and Nagasaki.

THE LAST STAGES OF WAR:
- Explain what significant changes developed in the last stages of the war.
- Describe the Holocaust and how Roosevelt, journalists, members of the military, and the American public reacted to it.
- Outline Truman's military and diplomatic reasons for U.S. use of the atomic bomb.
- **Identify:** the "Big Three," Patton, Buchenwald, the Yalta Conference, Atlantic Charter, "spheres of influence," Potsdam

CONCLUSION:
- Describe the human cost of World War II, both military and civilian, and compare it to earlier wars.

REVIEW QUESTIONS: Use these to check your grasp of the major chapter themes. It is good practice to write out essay answers to these questions.

STUDY SKILLS EXERCISES

1. Vocabulary:

fascist, p. 770	internment, p. 783
entanglements, p. 772	conscripts, p. 787
espionage, p. 776	stevedore, p. 789
militant, p. 780	partisans, p. 795
animosity, p. 783	logistics, p. 797

2. Making connections:
- What was the continued struggle of African Americans against segregation beginning during Reconstruction through the war years? What would be the answer to Langston Hughes's question, "How long I got to fight/ *BOTH HITLER—AND JIM CROW*"?
- Compare the U.S. involvement in and effects of World War I and World War II in terms of foreign and domestic policies.

3. Reflections: How do you think you would have reacted to the following U.S. policies in the World War II era?

- the Neutrality Acts
- changing the Neutrality Acts to Lend-Lease and other programs
- internment of Japanese Americans
- the policy toward Holocaust victims
- the summer of 1943 race riots
- Yalta and Potsdam
- U.S. development and use of the atomic bomb

RECITE/REVIEW

REVIEW QUESTIONS: This section has a sampling of multiple choice, short essay, and extended essay questions that you should be able to answer when you have completed the chapter and used other study techniques. To help you in reviewing the material, questions have been grouped according to the major sections of the chapter. Of course, you cannot expect your tests to be set up in this way.

▶ AMERICAN COMMUNITIES ◀

Multiple Choice

1. The Los Alamos Community was an example of a
   - a. Japanese American internment camp.
   - b. unique group of scientists working on war research.
   - c. new training base built in the West.
   - d. scene of zoot-suit rioting.

2. Roosevelt set up the bomb project because he feared that THIS country was working on it:
   - a. Japan.
   - b. the Soviet Union.
   - c. Nazi Germany.
   - d. Fascist Italy.

▶ THE COMING OF WORLD WAR II ◀

Multiple Choice

3. In a foreshadowing of what was to come, the Japanese army invaded THIS area early in 1931:
   - a. Korea.
   - b. Okinawa.
   - c. Thailand.
   - d. Manchuria.

4. This American opposition group to war was most well known because of famous personalities who were members, such as Henry Ford, Charles Lindbergh, and Lillian Gish:
   - a. America First.
   - b. Keep America Out of War Congress.
   - c. American League against War and Fascism.
   - d. Nye Committee.

5. Which one of the following was NOT an action the United States took before its formal entry into World War II?
   - a. meeting with Britain to draw up Atlantic Charter principles
   - b. a lend-lease policy to Britain and the Soviet Union
   - c. U.S. ships to shoot on sight any Nazi ship in U.S. "defensive waters"
   - d. asking the League to "quarantine the aggressors"

6. In addition to Pearl Harbor, the Japanese attacked all of the following on December 7, 1941 EXCEPT
   - a. Vietnam.
   - b. the Philippines.
   - c. Guam.
   - d. Wake Island.

Short Essay

7. How did FDR prepare the United States for another World War?

Extended Essay

8. Explain America's sentiment of isolationism and indicate how it shifted in the period from 1930 until Pearl Harbor.

▶ ARSENAL OF DEMOCRACY ◀

Multiple Choice

9. The War Powers Act gave a great deal of power to this section of the government to carry on the war:
    a. Congress.
    b. the president.
    c. the joint chiefs of staff.
    d. the secretary of war.

10. The CPI was to World War I as THIS was to World War II:
    a. OWI.
    b. NWLB.
    c. OSS.
    d. FBI.

11. The war had the greatest impact on the wage-earning patterns of
    a. Mexicans.
    b. Indians.
    c. white women.
    d. African American men.

12. Which one of the following strikes occurred in 1943 over the hiring of African American women?
    a. North American Aviation
    b. U.S. Rubber Company
    c. Allis-Chalmers
    d. Ford Motor Company

Short Essay

13. Describe the effect of World War II on organized labor.

Extended Essay

14. In what ways did the economic power of the United States help it to win World War II?

▶THE HOME FRONT◀

Multiple Choice

15. World War II had all of the following effects at home EXCEPT
    a. lowering the median age of first marriage for women.
    b. increasing high school enrollment.
    c. improving public health.
    d. increasing the growing of food in home gardens.

16. The focus of activity by the Congress of Racial Equality in the 1940s was on
    a. discrimination in the armed forces.
    b. equal employment opportunities.
    c. fair housing.
    d. segregation in public facilities.

17. Langston Hughes's question "How long I got to fight/*BOTH HITLER—AND JIM CROW*" was given organization by the African American
    a. "2nd Front" campaign.
    b. Victory Garden crusade.
    c. "Double V" campaign.
    d. Arsenal of Democracy program.

18. The zoot-suit riots were started by uniformed sailors assaulting youth from THIS community:
    a. Japanese American.
    b. Italian American.
    c. Mexican American.
    d. African American.

Short Essay

19. How were the civil rights of Japanese Americans violated during World War II?

Extended Essay

20. How did popular culture aid in the war effort?

▶ MEN AND WOMEN IN UNIFORM ◀

Multiple Choice

21. What percent of Americans enlisted in the armed forces saw combat?
    a. 52 percent   c. 34 percent
    b. 23 percent   d. 66 percent

22. The Nisei 442 Infantry was to Japanese Americans as the 99th Pursuit Squadron was to
    a. women.   c. Mexican Americans.
    b. German Americans.   d. African Americans.

23. Most medics in the army were recruited from
    a. conscientious objectors.   c. women.
    b. homosexuals.   d. trained physicians.

24. The "Death March" was the march of
    a. Russian POWs to German prisoner camps.
    b. American POWs across the Bataan Peninsula.
    c. American soldiers suffering from battle fatigue to field hospitals.
    d. Japanese POWs to Bilibid Prison in Manila.

Map Question

25. While military facilities were in many parts of the United States, new construction for World War II particularly benefited THESE areas:
    a. the Midwest and New England.
    b. U.S. territories in the Caribbean and the Pacific.
    c. the Great Plains—both south and north.
    d. the South and the West.

Short Essay

26. What role did women play in the U.S. war effort?

Extended Essay

27. How did service in the armed forces affect the lives of various minority groups?

▶The World at War◀

Multiple Choice

28. The first major setback for the Nazis occurred at
    a. Kursk.
    b. Stalingrad.
    c. Moscow.
    d. the Suez Canal.

29. Which one of the following Allied efforts had no military value?
    a. battle at El Alamein
    b. campaign in Morocco and Tunisia
    c. invasion of Italy
    d. bombing of Dresden

30. This counterattack was the bloodiest single American campaign since Gettysburg:
    a. Stalingrad.
    b. Battle of the Bulge.
    c. El Alamein.
    d. Okinawa.

31. Which one of the following statements is NOT true?
    a. In 1945, Britain and the United States were eager for the Soviet Union to invade Japan.
    b. The Battle of Leyte Gulf gave the United States control of the Pacific.
    c. There were more American casualties on Okinawa than at Normandy.
    d. The taking of Guam allowed U. S. bombers to reach Tokyo.

Map Questions

32. The first Allied victory in the Pacific after Pearl Harbor occurred in
    a. Corregidor.
    b. the Philippines.
    c. Guadalcanal.
    d. the Coral Sea.

33. The Americans followed this strategy in the Pacific to avoid sustained battle for each and every area the Japanese held:
    a. island hopping.
    b. wildcat.
    c. second front.
    d. Double V.

34. If you were a U.S. soldier and part of the D-Day invasion, where would you be landing?
    a. Sicily
    b. Normandy
    c. North Africa
    d. the Philippines

35. The easternmost victory of the Allies during the war in Europe occurred at
    a. El Alamein.
    b. Leningrad.
    c. Stalingrad.
    d. the Kasserine Pass.

Short Essay

36. What was the significance of the Second Front in Europe and how did it develop?

Extended Essay

37. What factors led to the United States having the upper hand in the war in the Pacific?

▶ THE LAST STAGES OF WAR ◀

Multiple Choice

38. Roosevelt and his advisers followed this policy in relation to Holocaust death camps:
    a. it was propaganda similar to World War I fabrications.
    b. total Allied victory was the best way to liberate camps.
    c. civilian rescue would be employed to distract the enemy.
    d. Soviet troops were closer and could liberate the camps.

39. Although this policy was unspoken, the United States and Britain accepted this area as a Soviet sphere of influence:
    a. areas of Manchuria and Korea.
    b. the Middle East.
    c. the Baltic states and part of Poland.
    d. certain Japanese islands.

Short Essay

40. Why did FDR avoid allocating U.S. military resources to stopping the Holocaust?

Extended Essay

41. Explain how the meetings at Yalta and Potsdam led to the American decision to use the atomic bomb in Japan.

▶ CONCLUSION ◀

Multiple Choice

42. While lower than other allies, the human cost of World War II for Americans was second only to
    - a. the American Revolution.
    - b. Vietnam.
    - c. World War I.
    - d. the Civil War.

▶ CHRONOLOGY QUESTIONS ◀

Multiple Choice

43. Which one of the following was NOT seized by Hitler from 1938 to 1939?
    - a. Belgium
    - b. Czechoslovakia
    - c. Austria
    - d. Poland

44. From 1935 to 1937, the United States tried to adhere to THESE in order to avoid involvement in a war as they did in World War I:
    - a. Quarantine Acts.
    - b. Atlantic Charter Principles.
    - c. Neutrality Acts.
    - d. Lend-Lease Acts.

45. Japan invaded China in
    - a. 1933.
    - b. 1935.
    - c. 1937.
    - d. 1941.

46. Roosevelt's executive order to remove Japanese Americans from the Pacific coast states to inland camps was issued in
    - a. 1937.
    - b. 1941.
    - c. 1942.
    - d. 1944.

American Communities
    1. b, p. 769
    2. c, p. 769

The Coming of World War II
    3. d, p. 771
    4. a, p. 772
    5. d, pp. 772–774
    6. a, p. 775
    7. pp. 772–774
    8. pp. 772–775

Arsenal of Democracy
    9. b, p. 776
    10. a, p. 776
    11. c, p. 778
    12. b, p. 780
    13. p. 780
    14. pp. 777–778

The Home Front
    15. b, pp. 781–782
    16. d, p. 784
    17. c, pp. 784–785
    18. c, p. 785
    19. pp. 782–783
    20. pp. 785–786

Men and Women in Uniform
    21. c, p. 786
    22. d, p. 789
    23. a, p. 790
    24. b, p. 791
    25. d, p. 787
    26. pp. 778–779, 788–789
    27. pp. 789–790

The World at War
    28. c, p. 792
    29. d, p. 794
    30. b, p. 796
    31. a, p. 798
    32. d, p. 797
    33. a, p. 797
    34. b, p. 793
    35. c, p. 793
    36. pp. 794–795
    37. pp. 797–798

The Last Stages of War
    38. b, pp. 798–799
    39. c, p. 799
    40. pp. 798–799
    41. pp. 799–800

Conclusion
    42. d, p. 800

Chronology Questions
    43. a, p. 801
    44. c, p. 801
    45. c, p. 801
    46. c, p. 801

CHAPTER 26 — The Cold War, 1945–1952

SURVEY

Chapter Overview: This chapter covers the beginnings of the Cold War under the Truman presidency as it affected both foreign and domestic policies. Peace after World War II was marred by a return to the 1917 rivalry of the United States and the Soviet Union. Truman and his advisors introduced the basic Cold War policies of containment in the Truman Doctrine, the Marshall Plan, and the North Atlantic Treaty Organization. With the victory of the communists in China and the outbreak of the Korean War, America extended the Cold War to Asia as well. The Cold War prompted the United States to rebuild its World War II enemies, Germany and Japan, as counterweights to the Soviets. At home, Americans wanted to return to normal by bringing the troops back home, spending for consumer goods, and re-establishing family life, but many changing social patterns brought anxieties. A second Red Scare was caused by the Cold War rhetoric of a bipartisan foreign policy and Truman's loyalty program, but Senator Joseph McCarthy's tactics symbolized the era. Defense spending increased and the American economy became dependent on it to maintain recovery. Truman tried to extend elements of the New Deal in his Fair Deal but with minimal success.

Before you begin reading, turn to the CHRONOLOGY at the end of the chapter. Review it to orient yourself in space and time and understand who the leading characters are in the story this chapter will tell. Look for cause and effect relationships. Note unfamiliar terms that you will be learning about. Use the tips and questions at the beginning of Chapter 17 of the Study Guide as a guide for your use of the time line. Return to the CHRONOLOGY after you have read the chapter to see how much you have learned.

QUESTIONS/READ

As you read each section, use the questions to help you focus on the major themes. Use them as a way to organize note-taking as you read. The objective is for you to be able to answer these questions after you have read the chapter and completed the study skills exercises. Be on the lookout for important terms that you should be able to identify (see the study skills section in Chapter 18 of the Study Guide for tips on how to fully identify these important terms), and do the map exercises as you go along.

AMERICAN COMMUNITIES:
- Illustrate the effects of the Red Scare by discussing the college campus community after World War II.
- **Identify:** Dr. Rader, Cold War, "red propaganda," Servicemen's Readjustment Act, loyalty acts

GLOBAL INSECURITIES AT WAR'S END:
- Explain why global insecurity existed at the war's end and identify the era that it actually dated back to.

- Trace America's growth into a major military and economic power after World War II.
- Describe the division of Europe after World War II and its role in helping or hurting the chances for peace.
- **Identify:** Bretton Woods, International Bank for Reconstruction and Development, International Monetary Fund, United Nations, General Assembly, Security Council, Eleanor Roosevelt, Dumbarton Oaks and San Francisco Conferences, International Court of Justice, Nuremberg trials, Nuremberg Principle, Churchill's iron curtain, Yugoslavia, Albania

THE POLICY OF CONTAINMENT:
- Trace the development of the American policy of containment as applied to Europe and to Asia.
- **Identify:** the Truman Doctrine, George Kennan, George Marshall, the Marshall Plan, General Agreement on Tariffs and Trades, the Berlin Crisis, NATO, Operation Vittles, Warsaw Pact, Senator Taft, East and West Germany, Bikini Islands, hydrogen bombs, nuclear arms race
- **Map exercise:** *Divided Europe:* (p. 815) What countries were in the NATO organization? Which ones were in the Warsaw Pact? How was Germany divided or occupied? Be able to locate or name all the countries shown on the blank map.

COLD WAR LIBERALISM:
- Summarize the foreign and domestic policies of the Truman administration. This theme draws from the previous section as well.
- Outline the major issues and the positions of various candidates in the elections of 1948.
- Compare the ideas and theories of the Fair Deal and the New Deal.
- **Identify:** "To Err Is Truman," Taft-Hartley Act, Americans for Democratic Action, Henry Wallace, Progressive party, "do-nothing Congress," Strom Thurmond's Dixiecrats
- **Map exercise:** *The Election of 1948:* (p. 818) Where was Truman's strength? Dewey's? What was the result of Strom Thurmond's candidacy?

THE COLD WAR AT HOME:
- Discuss the major causes, personalities, and events of the Red Scare.
- **Identify:** House Un-American Activities Committee, Tom Clark, Joseph R. McCarthy, National Security Act of 1947, Executive Order 9835, Pentagon, Internal Security Act, Immigration and Nationality Act, Subversive Activities Control Board, *Red Channels,* blacklist, Alger Hiss, Richard Nixon, Whittaker Chambers, Pumpkin Papers, the Rosenbergs, McCarthyism, Roy Cohn, Dean Acheson, W. E. B. Du Dois, Guy Gabrielson, J. Edgar Hoover, Howard McGrath, Arthur Schlesinger, Jr.

COLD WAR CULTURE:
- Explain the development of Cold-War-era anxiety and its reflection in American society and in popular culture.
- Describe how the baby boom and high rates of consumer spending changed the middle-class family.
- Outline the impact of the Cold War on the Trans-Mississippi West.
- **Identify:** *The Best Years of Our Lives, film noir, Death of a Salesman, Catcher in the Rye,* UFOs, baby boom, Lundberg, Farnham, Parsons, Spock, J. Edgar Hoover, GI Bill,

"American Woman's Dilemma," Waste Isolation Pilot Project, White Sands Missile Range, Zeal for Democracy, Samuel Eliot Morison, Richard Hofstader

END OF THE DEMOCRATIC ERA:
- Outline the events of the Korean War and its effect on American foreign policy and the political fortunes of Truman and the Democratic Party.
- **Identify:** Asia First, Jiang Jeishi, Mao Zedong, People's Republic of China, Syngman Rhee, Kim Il Sung, Douglas MacArthur, Inchon, Yalu River, 38th parallel, Robert Taft, "police action," NSC-68, Voice of America, *M★A★S★H,* Ring Lardner, Jr., Dwight D. Eisenhower, Adlai Stevenson, K1C2, Richard Nixon, Checkers speech
- **Map exercise:** *The Korean War:* (p. 831) Be able to locate the 38th parallel, Pusan, Inchon, Seoul, Pyongyang, Panmunjom, the Yalu River, and the Armistice Line.

CONCLUSION:
- Explain the meaning of the "Eisenhower Movement" and how it related to Cold War anxiety.
- Discuss the long-term effects of Cold War defense spending on American society.

REVIEW QUESTIONS: Use these to check your grasp of the major chapter themes. It is good practice to write out essay answers to these questions.

STUDY SKILLS EXERCISES

1. Vocabulary:

disavowal, p. 808	filibusters, p. 819
bilateral, p. 814	tandem, p. 832

2. Making connections:
- Compare American foreign and domestic policy in the postwar 1920s with the policies of the postwar 1940s.
- Compare the Red Scare after World War I to the one after World War II. (Chapter 23 and Chapter 26)

3. Reflection:
- If you had been president at the end of World War II, how would you have responded to the Soviets?
- How would you have voted in the 1948 election?
- Would you have been in favor of the Fair Deal?

RECITE/REVIEW

REVIEW QUESTIONS: This section has a sampling of multiple choice, short essay, and extended essay questions that you should be able to answer when you have completed the chapter and used other study techniques. To help you in reviewing the material, questions have been grouped according to the major sections of the chapter. Of course, you cannot expect your tests to be set up in this way.

▶ AMERICAN COMMUNITIES ◀

Multiple Choice

1. The main effect of Red Hysteria on college campuses was the
   a. restraint of free speech.
   b. decline of enrollment.
   c. increasing radicalism of students.
   d. increase in racism on campuses.

▶ GLOBAL INSECURITIES AT WAR'S END ◀

Multiple Choice

2. Which one of the following took place AFTER the end of World War II in Europe?
   a. Bretton Woods meeting
   b. Dumbarton Oaks Conference
   c. Potsdam Conference
   d. Atlantic Charter

3. What did these five countries have in common: United States, Great Britain, the Soviet Union, France, and Nationalist China?
   a. membership in NATO
   b. permanent members of the United Nations Security Council
   c. seats on the International Court of Justice
   d. members of the General Agreement on Tariffs and Trade

Short Essay

4. What were the strengths and weaknesses of the United Nations?

▶ THE POLICY OF CONTAINMENT ◀

Multiple Choice

5. Which one of the following would be LEAST likely to agree with the others on America's post-war role?
   a. Henry R. Luce
   b. George F. Kennan
   c. Winston Churchill
   d. Robert Taft

6. The Truman Doctrine was first applied to these countries:
   a. North and South Korea.
   b. East and West Germany.
   c. Turkey and Greece.
   d. Yugoslavia and Albania.

7. Which one of the following was NOT built around the policy of the containment of communism?
   a. the UN Charter
   b. the Marshall Plan
   c. the formation of NATO
   d. the Truman Doctrine

Map Questions

8. Which one of the following countries was NOT a member of NATO?
   a. Turkey
   b. Italy
   c. Norway
   d. Spain

9. All of the following Communist countries were part of the Warsaw Pact EXCEPT
   a. East Germany.
   b. Albania.
   c. Yugoslavia.
   d. Romania.

Short Essay

10. Describe the major goals of U.S. foreign policy toward the Soviet Union in the years directly following the end of World War II.

11. What were the effects of the Marshall Plan?

Extended Essay

12. Evaluate the over-all success (or failure) of the Truman Doctrine.

13. How did the United States attempt to align western European nations with it against the Soviet Union after World War II?

▶ COLD WAR LIBERALISM ◀

Multiple Choice

14. Which one of the following had the LEAST to do with trying to establish U.S. primacy in the postwar global economy?
    - a. World Bank
    - b. International Monetary Fund
    - c. Council of Economic Advisors
    - d. Marshall Plan

15. Which one of the following would be the MOST likely to support the Taft-Hartley Act?
    - a. Philip Murray
    - b. Walter Reuther
    - c. Henry Wallace
    - d. Thomas Dewey

16. Which one of the following did NOT help Truman win the election of 1948?
    - a. desegregating the armed forces
    - b. formation of the Americans for Democratic Action
    - c. success of the Berlin airlift
    - d. Henry Wallace's desire to work in harmony with the Soviet Union

Map Question

17. The states that Truman lost to Strom Thurmond in 1948 were located in
    - a. New England.
    - b. the South.
    - c. the Great Plains.
    - d. the Great Lakes area.

Extended Essay

18. What caused the economic problems that existed in the United States directly after World War II?

▶ THE COLD WAR AT HOME ◀

Multiple Choice

19. Statistically, the national security state had 10 percent of federal employees before World War II. After the war, the federal work force in national security was
    - a. 25 percent.
    - b. 35 percent.
    - c. 50 percent.
    - d. 75 percent.

20. President Truman's Executive Order 9835
    - a. desegregated the armed forces.
    - b. brought combat troops home rapidly from WWII.
    - c. ended the wartime price and rationing controls.
    - d. established a federal employee loyalty program.

21. Which one of the following was LEAST likely to go along with the smear tactics of the Red Scare?
    a. Dean Acheson
    b. Roy Cohn
    c. Joseph McCarthy
    d. J. Edgar Hoover

22. Which one of the following historians would have been MOST likely to have angered Joseph McCarthy?
    a. W. E. B. Du Bois
    b. Samuel Eliot Morison
    c. Richard Hofstader
    d. Arthur M. Schlesinger, Jr.

23. Which one of the following was called "the greatest danger to freedom of press, speech, and assembly since the Sedition Act of 1798" by President Truman?
    a. the National Security Act of 1947
    b. the Federal Employees Loyalty and Security Program
    c. the Internal Security (McCarran) Act
    d. the Immigration and Nationality Act

Short Essay
24. What was the purpose of the House Committee on Un-American Activities?

Extended Essay
25. How did the National Security Act of 1947 lead to infringement of civil rights?

▶ COLD WAR CULTURE ◀

Multiple Choice
26. What was the effect of the GI bill on women?
    a. lessened their chances of federal employment
    b. decreased their enrollment in college
    c. forced them into the service sector rather than manufacturing
    d. increased their reliance on electrical appliances

27. The 1947 federal "Zeal for Democracy" program promoted strengthening national security and fighting Soviet communism through
    a. education.
    b. the family.
    c. women staying home.
    d. religion.

28. An example of the age of Cold War anxiety was the popularity of the movie
    a. *They Live by Night.*   c. *The Invasion of the Body Snatchers.*
    b. *I Married a Communist.*   d. *Red Channels.*

29. Which one of the following statements is true?
    a. Women provided half the growth of the total labor force after World War II.
    b. Women continued to work in unionized manufacturing jobs after World War II.
    c. The same number of wives worked after the war as during it.
    d. Mothers of young children were the least likely to be employed after World War II.

30. Which one of the following states had the HIGHEST proportion of its state income from federal military dollars during the Cold War?
    a. California
    b. New Mexico
    c. Texas
    d. Utah

Short Essay

31. How were women's roles connected to the fight against communism during the Cold War?

Extended Essay

32. What were the effects of increased defense spending on the communities of the West during the Cold War?

▶ END OF THE DEMOCRATIC ERA ◀

Multiple Choice

33. The Asia First wing of the Republican Party referred to the Democrats as a "party of treason" because of Truman's
    a. giving independence to the U.S. possession of the Philippines.
    b. failing to support MacArthur's views in the Korean War.
    c. breaking off relations with China's Jiang.
    d. post-war policies in Japan.

34. As far as Truman was concerned, this Asian country and its situation was like that of Greece when he proclaimed his Truman Doctrine:
    a. the Philippines.
    b. China.
    c. Vietnam.
    d. Korea.

35. The Korean War began when
    a. North Korea launched a military attack on South Korea.
    b. Communist China invaded Korea to keep the Nationalist Chinese out.
    c. the Soviet Union joined its North Korean ally in invasion.
    d. South Korea attempted to unify both occupation zones of Korea.

36. Truman derived his authority to commit the United States to war in Korea from
    a. a congressional declaration of war.
    b. the NATO charter.
    c. a National Security Council paper.
    d. recommendation of the Joint Chiefs of Staff.

37. All of the following were the result of the Korean War EXCEPT
    a. quadrupling of the defense budget.
    b. strengthening the case of the United States for rolling back communism.
    c. expanding anti-Communist propaganda.
    d. the deaths of 2 million North Koreans and Chinese.

38. The Republican formula for attacking Truman and the Democrats in the 1952 election was K_1C_2, meaning Korea, communism, and
    a. country.
    b. containment.
    c. Checkers.
    d. corruption.

Map Questions

39. Where did UN forces land to begin their counterattack in September 1950?
    a. Pyongyang
    b. Inchon
    c. Seoul
    d. Pusan

40. Which one of the following cities is located on the armistice line between North and South Korea?
    a. Pyongyang
    b. Panmunjom
    c. Seoul
    d. Inchon

Short Essay

41. Why did Truman feel compelled to act in South Korea?

Extended Essay

42. Analyze China's role in the Korean War.

▶ CHRONOLOGY QUESTIONS ◀

Multiple Choice

43. Which one of the following gives the correct chronological order of these events?

    (1) formation of NATO   (3) Berlin Crisis
    (2) the Truman Doctrine   (4) Korean War

    a. 3, 2, 4, 1   c. 2, 3, 1, 4
    b. 2, 4, 3, 1   d. 4, 3, 1, 2

44. In 1949, these two events occur that increase the Cold War anxiety of the United States:

    a. China becomes Communist and the Soviet Union explodes an atomic bomb.
    b. the Soviet Union and China ally and the Korean War begins.
    c. HUAC hearings are held in Hollywood and the Soviets blockade Berlin.
    d. the Marshall Plan and Truman Doctrine are enacted.

45. Truman dismisses MacArthur and Armistice talks begin in Korea in

    a. 1950.   c. 1952.
    b. 1951.   d. 1953.

46. The period from the House Un-American Activities Committee hearings to the end of the Army-McCarthy hearings was

    a. 1950–1954.
    b. 1950–1952.
    c. 1947–1954.
    d. 1947–1950.

ANSWERS–CHAPTER 26

American Communities
1. a, pp. 808–809

Global Insecurities at War's End
2. c, p. 811
3. b, p. 812
4. p. 812

The Policy of Containment
5. d, pp. 810, 812
6. c, p. 813
7. a, pp. 812–815
8. d, p. 815
9. c, p. 815
10. pp. 812–814
11. p. 814
12. pp. 812–814
13. pp. 814–815

Cold War Liberalism
14. c, pp. 811, 814, 816
15. d, pp. 817–818
16. a, pp. 817–818
17. b, p. 818
18. p. 816

Cold War at Home
19. d, p. 820
20. d, p. 820
21. a, pp. 819, 823
22. a, pp. 823, 828
23. c, p. 821
24. p. 822
25. pp. 820–821

Cold War Culture
26. b, pp. 825–826
27. a, p. 828
28. c, p. 824
29. a, p. 825
30. d, p. 827
31. p. 826
32. pp. 827–828

End of the Democratic Era
33. c, p. 829
34. d, p. 830
35. a, p. 829
36. c, p. 831

37. b, p. 832
38. d, p. 833
39. b, p. 831
40. b, p. 831
41. pp. 829–830
42. p. 830

Chronology Questions
43. c, p. 834
44. a, p. 834
45. b, p. 834
46. c, p. 834

27 America at Mid-Century, 1952–1963

SURVEY

Chapter Overview: This chapter covers the changes in American society from 1945 to 1960. Although unevenly shared, America experienced great economic growth and affluence during the postwar era. More Americans owned homes, obtained college educations, and experienced an improved standard of living. On the negative side, the cities declined, racism remained entrenched, and the environment was damaged. A combination of public education, the baby boom, and affluence helped create the youth culture expressed in rock 'n' roll. At the same time, numerous critics objected to the development of mass culture of both youth and adults, especially the headlong pursuit of material comfort. Both Eisenhower and Kennedy would search for foreign policies that would continue the leadership of America, but they met with mixed success. Eisenhower refused to challenge New Deal programs and even extended some. Kennedy tried to revive the liberalism of the 1930s with his New Frontier.

Before you begin reading, turn to the CHRONOLOGY at the end of the chapter. Review it to orient yourself in space and time and understand who the leading characters are in the story this chapter will tell. Look for cause and effect relationships. Note unfamiliar terms that you will be learning about. Use the tips and questions at the beginning of Chapter 17 of the Study Guide as a guide for your use of the time line. Return to the CHRONOLOGY after you have read the chapter to see how much you have learned.

QUESTIONS/READ

As you read each section, use the questions to help you focus on the major themes. Use them as a way to organize note-taking as you read. The objective is for you to be able to answer these questions after you have read the chapter and completed the study skills exercises. Be on the lookout for important terms that you should be able to identify (see the study skills section in Chapter 18 of the Study Guide for tips on how to fully identify these important terms), and do the map exercises as you go along.

AMERICAN COMMUNITIES:
- Describe the music in Memphis that influenced Elvis Presley and how he contributed to the development of rock 'n' roll.
- Explain how rock 'n' roll helped create a new teenage community and define the nature of the youth culture.
- **Identify:** Beale Street, Midnight Rambles, Sam Phillips, Alan Freed

AMERICAN SOCIETY AT MID-CENTURY:
- Discuss the status of American society at mid-century and its major themes.
- Illustrate how the New Deal continued through the Eisenhower administration.
- **Identify:** *The Affluent Society,* Charles Wilson, Submerged Lands Act, Department of

Health, Education and Welfare, Oveta Culp Hobby, FHA, Veterans Act, Federal Highway Act, National Defense Education Act, Levittown, *The Feminine Mystique,* Norman Vincent Peale and Bishop Fulton J. Sheen, Centerless City, David Riesman, William H. Whyte, Sloan Wilson, C. Wright Mills, National Institute of Mental Health, Jonas Salk, AMA

YOUTH CULTURE:

- Describe the types of ideas and values that drove the youth culture and what types of problems there were.
- **Identify:** teenager, youth market, rock 'n' roll, Chuck Berry, cover versions, Alan Freed, "Sweet Little Sixteen," "Yakety Yak," "Summertime Blues," Marlon Brando and James Dean

MASS CULTURE AND ITS DISCONTENTS:

- Outline the basic elements of mass culture as well as the substance of attacks by critics of mass culture.
- Describe the relationship of television to politics.
- **Identify:** Estes Kevauver, Joseph McCarthy, Richard Nixon, the Beats, Jack Kerouac's *On the Road,* Allen Ginsberg's *Howl,* beatnik

THE COLD WAR CONTINUED:

- Trace the continuing events and policies of the Cold War through the Eisenhower administration.
- Describe the covert action by the CIA in Iran, Israel, the Suez, Guatemala, and Vietnam.
- **Identify:** spirit of Camp David, U-2 flights, Francis Gary Powers, Sputnik, Nikita Khrushchev, John Foster Dulles, Allen Dulles, Mossadegh, Riza Shah Pahlevi, Nasser, Aswan, Guzman, Ho Chi Minh, Dien Bien Phu, domino theory, Geneva Agreement, SEATO, Ngo Dinh Diem, the military-industrial complex
- **Map exercise:** *The U.S. in the Caribbean, 1948–1966:* (p. 857) What happened to U.S. intervention in the Caribbean after World War II? In which countries did the United States intervene? What dominated U.S. policy after 1960? Compare this map to the one on page 670, that covers 1865–1933. What countries was the United States consistently involved in?

JOHN F. KENNEDY AND THE NEW FRONTIER:

- Describe the candidates, issues, and outcome of the 1960 election.
- Trace the continuing events and policies of the Cold War through the Kennedy administration.
- Illustrate how the New Deal continued through the Kennedy administration.
- Compare the above themes with the Eisenhower administration.
- **Identify:** New Frontier, Apollo, Special Forces, Alliance for Progress, Bay of Pigs, Batista, Castro, Cuban missile crisis, hotline, Limited Nuclear Test Ban Treaty, Lyndon Johnson
- **Map exercise:** *Election of 1960:* (p. 861) Where did each candidate run the strongest? How did the popular vote of each candidate compare to the electoral vote? How close was the election?

CONCLUSION:

- Assess the status of the Cold War at the time of Kennedy's assassination.

REVIEW QUESTIONS: Use these to check your grasp of the major chapter themes. It is good practice to write out essay answers to these questions.

STUDY SKILLS EXERCISES

1. Vocabulary:

cloying, p. 840	counterinsurgency, p. 862
locus, p. 846	covert, p. 862
array, p. 852	syndicates, p. 863
burgeoning, p. 854	chastened, p. 864
tactical, p. 858	

2. Making connections:

- What trends of the 1920s (Chapter 23) do you see in the 1950s?
- How much do you think Woodrow Wilson (Chapter 21) and John Foster Dulles would have agreed on foreign policy?
- What significant roles did Eleanor Roosevelt continue to play in the postwar world? (Chapter 26)
- Analyze and evaluate American policies toward Latin America. (Chapters 20, 22, and 23)
- What points in this chapter do you still observe today in America?

3. Reflection:

- How would you have responded to rock 'n' roll?
- How would you have reacted to the critics of mass culture?
- What option would you have used in the Cuban Missile Crisis?
- What point of agreement was there between President Eisenhower and C. Wright Mills on the issue of power?

RECITE/REVIEW

REVIEW QUESTIONS: This section has a sampling of multiple choice, short essay, and extended essay questions that you should be able to answer when you have completed the chapter and used other study techniques. To help you in reviewing the material, questions have been grouped according to the major sections of the chapter. Of course, you cannot expect your tests to be set up in this way.

▶ AMERICAN COMMUNITIES ◀

Multiple Choice

1. Which one of the following was NOT part of the significance of rock 'n' roll?
    a. It was an expression of common identity for American youth.
    b. It helped encourage a teen community.
    c. It demonstrated the new buying power of American teens.
    d. It accelerated a separation of white and black music.

Multiple Choice

2. This new cabinet post was created under the Eisenhower administration:
   - a. Veterans Affairs.
   - b. Urban Affairs.
   - c. Health, Education and Welfare.
   - d. Defense.

3. The National Defense Education Act (NDEA) was a bipartisan effort led by Eisenhower in response to the Soviet
   - a. development of the hydrogen bomb.
   - b. launching the Sputnik satellite.
   - c. announcement of a manned space program.
   - d. U-2 spy flights.

4. Which one of the following is the RESULT of the other three?
   - a. passage of the Submerged Lands Act
   - b. degradation of Louisiana wetlands
   - c. increased role for the states in the oil business
   - d. Eisenhower favors businessmen for government appointments

5. In what way was Eisenhower's administration LEAST like the New Deal?
   - a. dismantled Social Security
   - b. discontinued subsidies to the housing industry
   - c. refused government spending to stimulate the economy
   - d. favored strong government regulation of industry

6. What did the FHA, Levittown, and the Federal Highway Act all have in common?
   - a. They were all established after World War II.
   - b. They all had a detrimental impact on the environment.
   - c. They all helped the revitalization of American cities.
   - d. They all contributed to the growth of suburbs.

7. Which one of the following did NOT characterize suburban life in the 1950s?
   - a. increase in church membership
   - b. reserved for college-educated, white collar employees
   - c. architectural and psychological conformity
   - d. the nuclear family as the ideal of American life

8. Which one of the following statements is NOT true?
   - a. the number of American doctors increased during 1950 and 1960
   - b. not all Americans shared equally in advances in medical care
   - c. Americans were living longer and healthier lives
   - d. most epidemic diseases were virtually eliminated from American life

Short Essay

9. What changes happened to organized labor in the 1950s and 1960s?

10. Describe the factors that led to the expansion of higher education in 1950s America.

Extended Essay

11. Analyze how Eisenhower's pre-presidential career shaped his presidency.

12. What were the criticisms leveled against postwar suburban America by various writers?

▶ YOUTH CULTURE ◀

Multiple Choice

13. Which one of the following was NOT an item that increased from 1945 to 1960?
    a. mobility and rental of homes
    b. number of people going to college
    c. suburbs and centerless cities
    d. disposable income of teenagers

14. Which one of the following has the LEAST in common with the others?
    a. Chuck Berry   c. Ray Charles
    b. Pat Boone   d. Alan Freed

15. Which one of the following statements is NOT true?
    a. By the 1950s, six out of eight teenagers went to high school.
    b. Locally produced radio replaced network programs in the 1950s.
    c. The dollar value of record sales nearly tripled between 1954 and 1959.
    d. Juvenile crime declined in the 1950s.

Short Essay

16. How did racism affect the growth of rock 'n' roll and the opposition to it?

Extended Essay

17. How did white teenagers in the 1950s and early 1960s exhibit both a new kind of youth orientation and a stronger identification with adult behavior?

▶ MASS CULTURE AND ITS DISCONTENTS ◀

Multiple Choice

18. Television shows like *Father Knows Best* and *Leave It to Beaver* were
    a. about working-class families struggling with the dilemmas of a consumer society.
    b. about the real problems of postwar families who had survived the Depression.
    c. urban ethnic shows based on old radio programs.
    d. idealized, affluent, suburban, WASP, middle-class programs.

19. Walt Disney's *Davy Crockett* series was a memorable example of television's ability to
    a. ignore real-life problems.
    b. create an overnight fad.
    c. rework old movie themes.
    d. indirectly influence a presidential election.

20. Vance Packard's *The Hidden Persuaders* charged this group with exploitation:
    a. the Central Intelligence Agency.
    b. television executives.
    c. advertisers.
    d. the military-industrial complex.

21. In his work *Growing Up Absurd*, Paul Goodman argued that
    a. it was hard for young people to find a true sense of community.
    b. juvenile delinquency was on the rise in suburban areas.
    c. television was a cancerous growth on American culture.
    d. rock 'n' roll was the "devil's music" and "a communicable disease."

Short Essay

22. Describe the relationship between television and the advertising industry.

23. In what ways was television apolitical in the 1950s?

▶ THE COLD WAR CONTINUED ◀

Multiple Choice

24. Eisenhower's Secretary of State, John Foster Dulles, called for a "new look" in American foreign policy that repudiated the
    a. heavy-handed interventionist diplomacy in Latin America.
    b. massive retaliation and atomic diplomacy of Truman.
    c. "spywars" and covert actions of the Truman administration.
    d. containment policy of Truman and Kennan.

25. When Nikita Khrushchev came to power, he made a goodwill gesture by withdrawing Soviet troops from
    a. Austria.
    b. Czechoslovakia.
    c. Cuba.
    d. East Berlin.

26. Eisenhower used the domino theory to justify America's
    a. military-industrial complex.
    b. containment policy in Asia.
    c. refusal to help seize the Suez Canal.
    d. covert CIA activity in Iran.

27. In the 1950s, groups like SANE, the Women's International League for Peace and Freedom, and the Student Peace Union conducted protests against
    a. the nuclear arms race.
    b. U.S. involvement in Vietnam.
    c. Eisenhower's refusal to stop the U-2 flights.
    d. Khrushchev's visit to the United States.

28. In which of the following countries did the CIA interfere with a local program of land reform in order to protect U.S. corporate interests?
    a. Egypt
    b. Guatemala
    c. Iran
    d. Vietnam

Map Questions

29. The United States tried to buy it in 1869, sent troops in from 1916–1924, financially supervised it from 1905–1941, and then sent in the U.S. Marines in 1965:
    a. Cuba.
    b. the Dominican Republic.
    c. Haiti.
    d. Guatemala.

30. The CIA-sponsored Bay of Pigs invasion of this country failed in 1961:
    a. Cuba.   c. Haiti.
    b. Panama.   d. Guatemala.

Short Essay

31. What was the military-industrial complex and what were the dangers of it that Eisenhower warned against?

Extended Essay

32. Describe U.S. foreign policy during the 1950s.

▶ JOHN F. KENNEDY AND THE NEW FRONTIER ◀

Multiple Choice

33. In its intentions, Kennedy's New Frontier originated from this previous program:
    a. Roosevelt's first Hundred Days New Deal.
    b. Roosevelt's second Hundred Days New Deal.
    c. Truman's Fair Deal.
    d. Eisenhower's "dynamic conservatism."

34. According to the authors, Kennedy's most long-lasting achievement as president was his
    a. striking a resonant chord with American youth.
    b. strengthening of the executive branch.
    c. New Frontier program.
    d. insistence on a manned space flight program.

35. Eisenhower's choice of Charles Wilson as his secretary of defense and Kennedy's choice of Robert McNamara as his secretary of defense both illustrate
    a. appointing auto executives to run the government like a business.
    b. an opposition to the dominance of the military-industrial complex.
    c. a governmental reliance on Ivy-League college graduates.
    d. appointing former military men as advisors in government.

36. When Khrushchev pledged to withdraw missiles from Cuba, Kennedy agreed to
    a. withdraw missiles from West Germany.
    b. set up a hotline for instant communication between them.
    c. sign a limited nuclear test ban agreement.
    d. respect Cuban sovereignty and not invade the island.

37. Which one of the following is NOT true?
    a. Kennedy expanded Eisenhower's policy of covert operations.
    b. Kennedy built up American nuclear and conventional weapons.
    c. Kennedy relied on advice that applied Cold War assumptions incorrectly.
    d. Kennedy consistently supported democracy rather than dictatorship in Latin America.

Map Questions

38. In the 1960 election, Kennedy's support was weakest in
    a. the South.   c. the West.
    b. southern New England. d. large northeastern cities.

39. Which one of the following clusters of states was won by Kennedy?
    a. Ohio, Indiana, and Kentucky
    b. North Carolina, South Carolina, and Georgia
    c. Maine, New Hampshire, and Vermont
    d. Michigan, Minnesota, and Iowa

Short Essay

40. How did Cold War assumptions affect Kennedy's foreign policy in Vietnam, Latin America, and Cuba?

Extended Essay

41. Contrast the political backgrounds of John Kennedy and Lyndon Johnson and analyze how Kennedy's background influenced his presidential governing style.

Multiple Choice

42. The CIA helped Riza Shah Pahlevi in Iran in
    a. 1953.
    c. 1956.
    b. 1954.
    d. 1961.

43. Which one of the following does NOT happen in 1960?
    a. Soviets shoot down a U-2 spy plane.
    b. John F. Kennedy is elected president.
    c. The Bay of Pigs invasion fails.
    d. Almost 90 percent of American homes have a television.

44. Rising star Elvis Presley signs with RCA in
    a. 1950.
    c. 1954.
    b. 1952.
    d. 1956.

45. Which one of the following lists the correct chronological order of events?
    (1) David Riesman's *The Lonely Crowd* is published.
    (2) Jack Kerouac's *On the Road* is published.
    (3) Alan Ginsberg's *Howl* is published.
    (4) Betty Friedan's *The Feminine Mystique* is published.

    a. 1, 4, 3, 2
    c. 3, 2, 4, 1
    b. 1, 3, 2, 4
    d. 1, 4, 3, 2

46. Which one of the following does NOT show a correct pairing of events that happened one year apart?
    a. Sputnik/National Defense Education Act
    b. Cuban Missile Crisis/Limited Nuclear Test Ban Treaty
    c. Presidential Commission on the Status of Women/*The Feminine Mystique*
    d. U-2 spy plane shot down/Kennedy creates "Green Berets"

American Communities
1. d, p. 840

American Society at Mid-Century
2. c, p. 842
3. b, p. 844
4. b, p. 842
5. c, p. 842
6. d, p. 843
7. b, pp. 844–845
8. a, p. 847
9. pp. 845–846
10. pp. 846–847
11. p. 842
12. pp. 844–846

Youth Culture
13. a, p. 843–848
14. b, p. 849
15. d, pp. 848–850
16. pp. 849–850
17. p. 850

Mass Culture and Its Discontents
18. d, p. 852
19. b, p. 852
20. c, p. 853
21. a, p. 853
22. pp. 851–852
23. pp. 852–853

The Cold War Continued
24. d, p. 854–855
25. a, p. 855
26. b, p. 858
27. a, p. 859
28. b, p. 858
29. b, p. 857
30. a, p. 857
31. pp. 859–860
32. pp. 854–856

John F. Kennedy and the New Frontier
33. b, p. 861
34. b, p. 862
35. a, p. 862
36. d, p. 864
37. d, pp. 862–863
38. c, p. 861

39. b, p. 861
40. pp. 863–864
41. pp. 860, 862

Chronology Questions
42. a, p. 866
43. c, p. 866
44. d, p. 866
45. b, p. 866
46. c, p. 866

The Civil Rights Movement, 1945–1966

SURVEY

Chapter Overview: This chapter covers the mass movements for civil rights beginning in the black community and then extending to the Mexican American, Puerto Rican, Asian, and American Indian communities as well. This era, often called the "Second Reconstruction," saw advances against segregation through federal court decisions and more direct activism as black leaders forced the larger community to face segregation issues. The Civil Rights Act of 1964 and the Voting Rights Act of 1965 reinforced political equality, but economic and social equality did not automatically follow. The persistence of poverty, entrenched racism, and ghetto slums brought a split in the black consensus over goals for their movement. The civil rights movement overall and the Great Society created new pride and expectation as well as anger and a more militant movement.

Before you begin reading, turn to the CHRONOLOGY at the end of the chapter. Review it to orient yourself in space and time and understand who the leading characters are in the story this chapter will tell. Look for cause and effect relationships. Note unfamiliar terms that you will be learning about. Use the tips and questions at the beginning of Chapter 17 of the Study Guide as a guide for your use of the time line. Return to the CHRONOLOGY after you have read the chapter to see how much you have learned.

QUESTIONS/READ

As you read each section, use the questions to help you focus on the major themes. Use them as a way to organize note-taking as you read. The objective is for you to be able to answer these questions after you have read the chapter and completed the study skills exercises. Be on the lookout for important terms that you should be able to identify (see the study skills section in Chapter 18 of the Study Guide for tips on how to fully identify these important terms), and do the map exercises as you go along.

AMERICAN COMMUNITIES:
- Explain how the Montgomery Bus Boycott drew an African American community together to challenge segregation.
- **Identify:** Rosa Parks, Martin Luther King, Jr., E. D. Nixon, Jo Ann Robinson, Montgomery Improvement Association, Women's Political Council

ORIGINS OF THE MOVEMENT:
- Discuss the origins of the civil rights movement in the postwar years to the crisis in Little Rock, Arkansas.
- Compare the attitudes and actions of Harry Truman and Dwight Eisenhower regarding civil rights.
- **Identify:** NAACP, Adam Clayton Powell, Jr., Thurgood Marshall, Congress of Racial Equality, *Morgan* v. *Virginia,* Freedom Ride, Jackie Robinson, Ralph Bunche, "bebop,"

Missouri v. *ex. rel. Gaines, McLaurin* v. *Oklahoma State Regents,* Earl Warren, *Brown* v. *Board of Education,* Little Rock, Orval Faubus, Southern Manifesto

NO EASY ROAD TO FREEDOM, 1957–1962:

- Explain why and how some black leaders pursued means other than the legal strategy followed by the NAACP.
- Outline the six key lessons Martin Luther King felt were learned from the bus boycott victory in Montgomery.
- Describe the role of civil rights in the election of 1960 and in the early years of the Kennedy administration. How did Kennedy compare with Eisenhower and Truman?
- **Identify:** SCLC, Walter Rauschenbusch, Mohandas Gandhi, "Beloved Community," sit-in tactic, Greensboro, Nashville and Atlanta, Rev. James Lawson, Julian Bond, Lonnie King, SNCC, Ella Baker, "minimum legislation, maximum executive action," Robert Kennedy, Civil Rights Act of 1957, Burke Marshall, Freedom Rides, James Farmer, the Albany Movement, Laurie Pritchett, James Meredith, Ross Barnett, University of Mississippi
- **Map exercise:** *Map of the Civil Rights Movement:* (p. 876) In general, where were the key battlegrounds in the civil rights movement? Be able to match each of these cities to the significant civil rights movement events that happened there. Be able to identify or match the event to the city. Be able to locate the cities and states on a blank map.

THE MOVEMENT AT HIGH TIDE, 1963–1965:

- Summarize the successes of the civil rights movement from the Montgomery Bus Boycott to the Voting Rights Act of 1965.
- Trace the record of Truman, Eisenhower, Kennedy, and Johnson in trying to change segregation.
- **Identify:** Eugene Connor, Fred Shuttlesworth, *Letter from Birmingham Jail,* Freedom Now, March on Washington, George Wallace, Medgar Evers, A. Philip Randolph, John Lewis, Walter Reuther, King's "I have a dream" speech, Civil Rights Act of 1964, Freedom Summer campaign, Bob Moses, Dave Dennis, MFDP, freedom schools, Neshoba County, Ruby Robinson, Malcolm X, Nation of Islam, Elijah Mohammed, *Autobiography of Malcolm X,* Organization of Afro-American Unity, Black Power, Selma, "Bloody Sunday," Pettus Bridge, the Voting Rights Act of 1965
- **Map exercise:** *Impact of the Voting Rights Act of 1965:* (p. 892) In general, what happened to voter registration among African Americans in the South between 1960 and 1971? Which state had the LOWEST percentage of registered black voters in 1960? Which state had the HIGHEST? Which state was the lowest in 1971? Which state was the highest in 1971?

FORGOTTEN MINORITIES, 1945–1965:

- Outline the issues and strategies followed by other minorities who were inspired by the black movement and also outline the improvements gained.
- **Identify:** LULAC, GI Forum, *Mendez* v. *Westminster,* Delgado case, Hernandez decision, *bracero, jojados,* "Operation Wetback," *la raza,* Puerto Ricans, the "great migration," Jones Act of 1917, *el barrio,* the BIA relocation program, "termination," House Concurrent Resolution 108, National Congress of American Indians, Native American Rights Fund, Indian Claims Commission, *United States* v. *Wheeler,* "ethnic Indians," National Indian Youth Council, Japanese Americans, JACL, the McCarran-Walter Act, Immigration and Nationality Acts of 1952 and 1965

CONCLUSION:

- Summarize the gains made by blacks and other minorities toward political or constitutional freedom.
- Describe the changes that were developing within black groups as well as white opposition groups by the mid-1960s.
- Describe Martin Luther King's broader vision.

REVIEW QUESTIONS: Use these to check your grasp of the major chapter themes. It is good practice to write out essay answers to these questions.

STUDY SKILLS EXERCISES

1. Vocabulary:

contingent, p. 871	mediators, p. 884
pivotal, p. 872	vigil, p. 886
epithets, p. 873	enjoined, p. 891
vilification, p. 880	chronic, p. 895

2. Making connections:

- Compare the *Plessy* v. *Ferguson* and Jim Crow laws (Chapter 19 and Chapter 21) with the changes made by the cases leading up to and including *Brown* v. *Board of Education*.
- How did the Brandeis brief (Chapter 21) help Thurgood Marshall?
- What are the similarities between the union tactic of the sit-down strike (Chapter 24) and the sit-in tactic?
- Compare the first period of Reconstruction and the era following up to *Plessy* v. *Ferguson* to the era after World War II with *Brown* v. *Board of Education* and a revived civil rights movement. (Chapter 17 and Chapter 19)

3. Reflection:

- Imagine yourself as an African American living in the South in the 1950s. What activist group, if any, would have appealed to you? Imagine yourself as a white person living in the South in the 1950s. What side would you take?
- What is the appeal of an idea like the "beloved community"? Is it possible to achieve?

RECITE/REVIEW

REVIEW QUESTIONS: This section has a sampling of multiple choice, short essay, and extended essay questions that you should be able to answer when you have completed the chapter and used other study techniques. To help you in reviewing the material, questions have been grouped according to the major sections of the chapter. Of course, you cannot expect your tests to be set up in this way.

▶ AMERICAN COMMUNITIES ◀

Multiple Choice

1. In 1955, the black community in Montgomery, Alabama represented this fraction of the city's population:
   - a. one tenth.
   - b. one fourth.
   - c. one third.
   - d. one half.

Multiple Choice

2. Which one of the following was NOT a step President Truman took that shifted most black voters to the Democratic Party?
   - a. a presidential committee on Civil Rights that made ambitious recommendations
   - b. Truman publicly endorsed the report *To Secure These Rights.*
   - c. He desegregated the armed forces by executive order.
   - d. He met with Thurgood Marshall and praised the NAACP.

3. Black jazz musicians created a more complex music in the forties that was harder for whites to copy, cover over, or sweeten. This music was called
   - a. bebop.
   - b. rockabilly.
   - c. rebop.
   - d. swing.

4. A combination of legal and violent acts kept all but the most determined blacks from voting in the late 1940s. The number was _____ percent.
   - a. 1
   - b. 5
   - c. 10
   - d. 15

5. The victory in *Brown* v. *Board of Education* was limited by this second ruling:
   - a. accepting the idea of "interposition" as a legal argument.
   - b. giving responsibility for implementation to local school boards.
   - c. monitoring would be decided by the local community.
   - d. schools would have a ten-year time plan to implement.

6. Which one of the following individuals is NOT matched correctly with his area of contribution to civil rights?
   - a. Adam Clayton Powell, Jr./UN diplomat
   - b. Thurgood Marshall/NAACP lawyer
   - c. Jackie Robinson/Major League Baseball player
   - d. Charlie Parker/jazz musician

7. Which one of the following has the LEAST in common with the other three?
   - a. *Morgan* v. *Virginia*
   - b. Fellowship of Reconciliation
   - c. Orville Faubus
   - d. Congress of Racial Equality

Short Essay

8. Explain the quotation attributed to a black preacher on page 874.

9. How did the events at Little Rock High School define the role of the federal government with respect to civil rights?

Extended Essay

10. Compare and contrast the attitudes and actions of Harry Truman and Dwight Eisenhower regarding desegregation.

▶No Easy Road to Freedom◀

Multiple Choice

11. Martin Luther King, Jr. was inspired by this American theologian's social Christianity:
    a. Walter Rauschenbusch.
    b. Ralph Abernathy.
    c. Billy Graham.
    d. Norman Vincent Peale.

12. Greensboro, North Carolina, Nashville, Tennessee, and Atlanta, Georgia were the sites of this particular strategy of the civil rights movement:
    a. Freedom Rides to test the *Morgan* v. *Virginia* ruling in interstate buses.
    b. mass signings of a southern manifesto to defeat segregation.
    c. sit-ins at lunch counters and restaurants to protest discrimination.
    d. voter registration drives to increase the number of black voters.

13. All of the following were leaders of the sit-in movement EXCEPT
    a. Reverend James Lawson.
    b. Marion Barry.
    c. Julian Bond.
    d. James Meredith.

14. If you were a young white southerner who supported the aims of SNCC, you might have joined the
    a. Albany Movement.
    b. Southern Christian Leadership Conference.
    c. Fellowship of Reconciliation.
    d. Southern Student Organizing Committee.

15. Which one of the following was NOT a strategy used by the Kennedy administration to support civil rights?
    a. appointment of African Americans to federal positions
    b. passed a new civil rights law to speed up desegregation
    c. established a Committee on Equal Employment Opportunity
    d. reinvigorated the Civil Rights Division of the Justice Department

Map Questions

16. Eisenhower sent troops to integrate a high school in
    a. Selma, Alabama.
    b. Atlanta, Georgia.
    c. Little Rock, Arkansas.
    d. Oxford, Mississippi.

17. The Freedom Ride to Mississippi met violence in
    a. Alabama.
    b. Georgia.
    c. Kansas.
    d. North Carolina.

Short Essay

18. What event thrust Martin Luther King, Jr. into the national spotlight and why? Describe King's involvement in this event.

19. What were the three groups that made up white southern society, and how did blacks use knowledge of these groups in their political strategy?

Extended Essay

20. What is the irony of the role the civil rights issue played in the 1960 presidential election? Why did this irony come about?

▶ THE MOVEMENT AT HIGH TIDE ◀

Multiple Choice

21. The Freedom Rides were to *Morgan* v. *Virginia* desegregation on interstate facilities as the Mississippi Freedom Summer was to
    a. voter registration.
    b. college registration.
    c. union organizing.
    d. job opportunities.

22. Which one of the following was NOT a crisis planned to arouse national indignation?
    a. Birmingham campaign
    b. Selma campaign
    c. March on Washington
    d. Albany Movement

23. Which one of the following has the LEAST to do with Malcolm Little?
    a. Nation of Islam
    b. Black Power
    c. Black Muslims
    d. "Bloody Sunday"

24. The Birmingham campaign resulted in all of the following EXCEPT
    a. increased black voter registration.
    b. unemployed African Americans and the working poor joined the protest.
    c. four girls were killed in a Baptist Church bombing.
    d. army troops were used to maintain order.

25. Which one of the following is the RESULT of the other three?
    a. Kennedy personally endorses civil rights activism.
    b. George Wallace blocks black students from entering the University of Alabama.
    c. The March on Washington is planned.
    d. Medgar Evers is assassinated.

26. Which one of the following wanted to publicly criticize the Kennedys' civil rights record?
    a. A. Philip Randolph
    b. John Lewis
    c. Walter Reuther
    d. Coretta Scott King

27. Which one of the following was NOT part of the Civil Rights Act of 1964?
    a. outlawed discrimination in employment
    b. financial aid for school desegregation
    c. prohibited discrimination in public accommodations
    d. eliminated literacy tests for voter registration

28. "Bloody Sunday" was part of
    a. the Freedom Summer.
    b. the Selma campaign.
    c. the Birmingham campaign.
    d. the March on Washington.

Map Questions

29. The Freedom Summer activists concentrated on this southern state since it had the lowest number of African American registered voters in 1960:
    a. Louisiana.
    b. South Carolina.
    c. Alabama.
    d. Mississippi.

30. Which one of the following states made the least progress in voter registration in the 1960s?
    a. Tennessee
    b. North Carolina
    c. South Carolina
    d. Florida

Short Essay

31. Describe the differences between lower-class black protestors and those who had been most active before the Birmingham campaign.

32. Describe Lyndon Johnson's role in passing the Civil Rights Act of 1964.

33. How did the Mississippi Freedom Summer test the ideal of the Beloved Community?

Extended Essay

34. Evaluate the relative successes and failures of the Birmingham campaign, Mississippi Freedom Summer, and Selma campaign.

35. Compare and contrast the roles of Martin Luther King, Jr. and Malcolm X in the black community.

▶ FORGOTTEN MINORITIES ◀

Multiple Choice

36. The Immigration and Nationality Act of 1965 ended
    a. the termination policy.
    b. national-origin quotas.
    c. Operation Wetback.
    d. Issei citizenship eligibility.

37. The NAACP was to pursuing legal cases in the black community as THIS group was to pursuing them in the Mexican American community:
    a. LULAC.
    b. La RAZA.
    c. BRACERO.
    d. ANMA.

38. The Jones Act of 1917 granted U.S. citizenship to
    a. Issei.
    b. Puerto Ricans.
    c. illegal Mexican immigrants.
    d. Native Americans not on reservations.

39. With the change in the Immigration and Nationality Act of 1965, this group was not the largest Asian-American group in 1985 as it had been in 1960:
    a. Chinese.
    b. Vietnamese.
    c. Japanese.
    d. Koreans.

40. Which one of the following court cases is NOT correctly matched with the topic of the decision?
    a. *United States* v. *Wheeler:* unique and limited sovereignty of Indian tribes
    b. *Mendez* v. *Westminste:* illegality of segregation of Mexican Americans
    c. *Missouri* v. *ex. rel. Gaines:* a separate law school must be fully equal
    d. *McLaurin* v. *Oklahoma State Regents:* black students must be admitted to law school

Short Essay
41. Describe the process of "termination" and its effects on American Indian tribes.

Extended Essay
42. Analyze the effect the black civil rights movement had on the movements to gain civil rights for other minority groups.

▶ CHRONOLOGY QUESTIONS ◀

Multiple Choice

43. Which one of the following lists the correct order of events?
    (1) Brown case rules segregated schools are inherently unequal
    (2) Executive Order 8802 forbids racial discrimination in defense industries
    (3) Truman issues executive order desegregating the armed forces
    (4) Morgan case rules segregation on interstate buses is unconstitutional

    a. 2, 3, 4, 1   c. 2, 3, 1, 4
    b. 2, 4, 3, 1   d. 2, 4, 1, 3

44. The Mississippi Freedom Democratic Party is denied seats at this presidential convention:
    a. 1952.   c. 1960.
    b. 1956.   d. 1964.

45. The time between *Morgan* v. *Virginia* and the Freedom Rides was
    a. ten years.   c. seven years.
    b. 15 years.   d. 23 years.

46. Which one of the following years was NOT one in which an important civil rights event took place in Alabama?
    a. 1955   c. 1957
    b. 1963   d. 1965

ANSWERS-CHAPTER 28

American Communities
   1. d, p. 870

Origins of the Movement
   2. d, p. 872
   3. a, p. 873
   4. c, p. 874
   5. b, p. 875
   6. a, pp. 872–873
   7. c, pp. 873, 876
   8. p. 874
   9. pp. 876–877
  10. pp. 872, 876–877

No Easy Road to Freedom
  11. a, p. 877
  12. c, p. 878
  13. d, pp. 878–879, 883
  14. d, pp. 877, 880, 883
  15. b, p. 881
  16. c, p. 876
  17. a, p. 876
  18. pp. 870, 877
  19. p. 878
  20. pp. 880–881

The Movement at High Tide
  21. a, p. 888
  22. d, pp. 883–885, 890
  23. d, pp. 889–891
  24. a, p. 884
  25. c, p. 885
  26. b, p. 886
  27. d, pp. 888, 892
  28. b, p. 891
  29. d, p. 892
  30. b, p. 892
  31. p. 885
  32. pp. 886–888
  33. pp. 888–889
  34. pp. 883–885, 888–890, 890–892
  35. pp. 877–878, 883–886, 889–890

Forgotten Minorities
  36. b, p. 896
  37. a, p. 893
  38. b, p. 894
  39. c, p. 896
  40. d, pp. 875, 893, 895
  41. p. 895
  42. pp. 893–896

Chronology Questions
  43. b, p. 897
  44. d, p. 897
  45. b, p. 897
  46. c, p. 897

CHAPTER 29

War Abroad, War at Home, 1965–1974

SURVEY

Chapter Overview: This chapter covers the Vietnam conflict, the longest and least successful war in American history. The period of the greatest involvement was from 1965 to 1974, and because of their policies, it became known as Johnson's war and Nixon's war. The war and actions against it diverted the domestic agendas of President Johnson and the student groups. Ironically, President Nixon proved not to be as conservative as expected in some social reform areas. He was also able to make a major foreign policy change with China and subsequently with the Soviet Union. The civil rights movement spurred other groups like college students, gays, women, Latinos, Asian Americans, and Indians. Both the war and the agendas of the various groups dominated the politics of both the 1968 and 1972 presidential elections. 1968 would be a turning point with the Tet offensive, which, while won by the Americans, shocked the nation because of the gap it illustrated between rosy predictions of winning and actual fact. Martin Luther King, Jr. and Robert F. Kennedy were assassinated. The 1968 Democratic Convention would be surrounded by great violence. The national mood was dismal and the events of the Nixon administration and Watergate did not rebuild any national community consensus.

Before you begin reading, turn to the CHRONOLOGY at the end of the chapter. Review it to orient yourself in space and time and understand who the leading characters are in the story this chapter will tell. Look for cause and effect relationships. Note unfamiliar terms that you will be learning about. Use the tips and questions at the beginning of Chapter 17 of the Study Guide as a guide for your use of the time line. Return to the CHRONOLOGY after you have read the chapter to see how much you have learned.

QUESTIONS/READ

As you read each section, use the questions to help you focus on the major themes. Use them as a way to organize note-taking as you read. The objective is for you to be able to answer these questions after you have read the chapter and completed the study skills exercises. Be on the lookout for important terms that you should be able to identify (see the study skills section in Chapter 18 of the Study Guide for tips on how to fully identify these important terms), and do the map exercises as you go along.

AMERICAN COMMUNITIES:
- Explain the spirit of community that college students and other groups were seeking in the 1960s.
- Compare the SDS agenda with that of President Johnson, and explain how the Vietnam War impacted both groups.
- **Identify:** Uptown, Students for a Democratic Society, Urban Renewal Act, Packinghouse Workers Union, Tom Hayden, Port Huron Statement

VIETNAM: AMERICA'S LONGEST WAR:

- Explain how the Vietnam War became Johnson's war in spite of previous American involvement.
- Discuss the role of the press in the Vietnam War.
- Describe the results of the war in terms of emotional and political fallout.
- **Identify:** Gulf of Tonkin resolution, Vietcong, Barry Goldwater, "war of attrition," Operation Rolling Thunder, the credibility gap, J. William Fulbright, *Arrogance of Power,* Morley Safer, Eric Sevareid, Harrison Salisbury

A GENERATION IN CONFLICT:

- Explain why the peace movement was viewed as a generational conflict and describe how it mobilized and spread.
- Describe the U. S. army during the Vietnam War and compare it to World War II.
- **Identify:** baby boomers, free speech movement, Mario Savio, counterculture, flower children, Haight-Ashbury, Timothy Leary, Beatles, folk music, Joan Baez, Bob Dylan, "Make Love, Not War," *The Greening of America,* Woodstock, teach-in, Dow Chemical Company, Daniel and Philip Berrigan, Selective Service Act, fragging, a white man's war
- **Map exercise:** *Anti-War Protests on College and University Campuses, 1967–1969:* (p. 910) Where were campus-based protests centered in the United States when they first began? Where did they spread? Where were most protests centered in western Europe?

WARS ON POVERTY:

- Explain why there was a new awareness of poverty in the 1960s and how the Great Society program proposed to deal with it.
- Describe the problems of cities in the 1960s that led to urban uprisings.
- **Identify:** Michael Harrington's *Other America,* OEO, Job Corps, Youth Corps, VISTA, CAP, Legal Services Program, Community Health Centers, Upward Bound, white flight, redlining, Negro removal, Watts, Newark and Detroit, the Kerner Commission
- **Map exercise:** *Urban Uprisings, 1965–1968:* (p. 915) What did rioters take aim at in their communities? In general, where were most urban uprisings? What states and cities experienced the most uprisings?

1968:

- Discuss why certain events of 1968 were pivotal in American domestic and foreign policies.
- **Identify:** the Tet Offensive, the "Beloved Community," Robert Kennedy, Eugene McCarthy, Hubert Humphrey, children's crusade, "the whole world is watching," Yippies, Abbie Hoffman, Richard Daley, McCarthy headquarters, police riot, Abraham Ribicoff, "Be Realistic, Demand the Impossible"
- **Map exercise:** *The Southeast Asian War:* (p. 917) Be able to locate South and North Vietnam and Cambodia. Where did the Tet Offensive take place? Locate the following: Gulf of Tonkin, Saigon, and Hanoi.

THE POLITICS OF IDENTITY:

- Trace the shift in the civil rights movement from King's leadership to the Black Power of Stokely Carmichael and others.
- Summarize the impact of the civil rights movement on other groups and outline the beliefs and agendas of these groups.

- **Identify:** the Establishment, Jesse Jackson, Operation Breadbasket, Black Panthers, Huey Newton and Bobby Seale, Black Power, cultural nationalism, Muhammed Ali, Kwanzaa, Black is Beautiful, Betty Friedan's *The Feminine Mystique,* National Organization for Women, consciousness-raising groups, Kate Millet's *Sexual Politics,* the Stonewall Riot, GLF, *Chicano, la raza,* Bilingual Education Act, Brown Berets, *Chicanismo,* Corky Gonzale's Crusade for Justice, Alcatraz, American Indian Movement, the Indian Renaissance, George Mitchell, Dennis Banks, Native American Rights Fund, AAPA, Gooks, *Woman Warrior, Sansei*
- **Map exercise:** *Major Indian Reservations, 1976:* (p. 926) Generally, where were most Indian reservations located in 1976? What states east of the Mississippi had reservations? Which of the eastern states had the largest number? Compare this map to the one on page 533 in Chapter 18. Which state(s) had increased areas of reservation in 1976 compared to the earlier map?

THE NIXON PRESIDENCY:
- Explain how the Vietnam War became Nixon's war in spite of previous American involvement.
- Describe the candidates, issues, and outcome of the 1968 election.
- **Identify:** the silent majority, Spiro T. Agnew, George Wallace, Kent State and Jackson State Universities, the Paris Peace Agreement of January 1973, Henry Kissinger, "Vietnamization," William L. Calley, the China Card, the Nixon Doctrine, the Nationalist Chinese government, "ping-pong diplomacy," SALT, shuttle diplomacy, Environmental Protection Agency, Occupational Safety and Health Administration, black capitalism, Warren Burger, *Apollo 11*
- **Map exercise:** *Election of 1968:* (p. 929) What area was won by George Wallace? What area that was traditionally Democratic from FDR days was lost by Democrats in 1968? Compare this to the map on page 861 to see exactly what states the Republicans won in 1968 that they had lost in 1960.

WATERGATE:
- Summarize the domestic and foreign policies of the Nixon administration and explain how the Watergate issue brought it to an end. Draw on the previous section for this answer as well.
- **Identify:** Anastazio Somoza, Salvador Allende, "dirty tricks," "plumbers," Daniel Ellsberg, Pentagon Papers, Watergate, E. Howard Hunt, G. Gordon Liddy, George McGovern, CREEP, Saturday Night Massacre, Gerald Ford

CONCLUSION:
- Describe the results of the Nixon and Agnew resignations on the national mood and the legacy of Watergate.
- **Identify:** War Powers Act

REVIEW QUESTIONS: Use these to check your grasp of the major chapter themes. It is good practice to write out essay answers to these questions.

STUDY SKILLS EXERCISES

1. Vocabulary:

mobilize, p. 903	turbulent, p. 917
subversion, p. 905	redlined, p. 919
resonated, p. 908	tenets, p. 920
inducements, p. 911	discord, p. 928
exodus, p. 914	surreptitious, p. 932

2. Making connections:

Chapters 27 and 28:

- Consider how the critics of mass culture like Paul Goodman and the Beat writers anticipated the counterculture and youth movement of the 1960s and how the energy of the civil rights movement added to it as well. Discuss how the war gave the counterculture more energy and yet diverted the goals of groups like the SDS in a search for meaningful community.

- Describe how music continued to provide identity.

- Compare the black activist views of Martin Luther King to those of Stokely Carmichael and Malcolm X.

- Consider the connection between Eisenhower's and Mill's warning of a military-industrial complex and student actions.

Chapters 26 and 27:

- Trace the involvement of the United States in Vietnam from the Truman to the Eisenhower to the Kennedy administrations, and connect this with the Johnson and Nixon administrations discussed in this chapter.

3. Reflections: If you had been on a college campus in 1965, how do you think you might have reacted to the escalation of the war? How would you have reacted if you were drafted? What type of reaction, mood, and feelings might you have had by the end of 1968? How might you have reacted if you were not on a campus?

RECITE/REVIEW

REVIEW QUESTIONS: This section has a sampling of multiple choice, short essay, and extended essay questions that you should be able to answer when you have completed the chapter and used other study techniques. To help you in reviewing the material, questions have been grouped according to the major sections of the chapter. Of course, you cannot expect your tests to be set up in this way.

▶ AMERICAN COMMUNITIES ◀

Multiple Choice

1. The carrying out of the Urban Renewal Act in the community of Uptown meant that the
   a. housing would be upgraded for middle-class families.
   b. government would help end poverty in the neighborhood.
   c. city would have civilian review boards to curb police harassment.
   d. citizens would be federally empowered to change their lives.

▶ VIETNAM: AMERICA'S LONGEST WAR ◀

Multiple Choice

2. Part of Johnson's motivation in being involved in Vietnam is that he did not want Vietnam to be to him as this was to Truman:
   - a. China and Korea.
   - b. the Soviet Union and East Germany.
   - c. Greece and Turkey.
   - d. Cuba and El Salvador.

3. Which one of the following was NOT a result of U.S. policy in Vietnam?
   - a. 4 million Vietnamese refugees
   - b. 3 million tons of bombs dropped
   - c. stabilization of the South Vietnamese government
   - d. the most destructive chemical warfare in history

Short Essay

4. What was meant by the "war of attrition" strategy and how successful was it?

Extended Essay

5. Analyze the role of television in influencing Americans' reactions to the war in Vietnam.

▶ A GENERATION IN CONFLICT ◀

Multiple Choice

6. The Free Speech Movement at the University of California in 1964 was created when university administrators tried to prevent students from
   - a. protesting the escalation of the war in Vietnam.
   - b. protesting segregation and other civil rights issues.
   - c. joining the United Farm Workers in a strike.
   - d. holding "teach-ins" and "be-ins."

7. The "teach-in" united these two movements:
   - a. student free speech and protesting the war.
   - b. civil rights and student demonstrations.
   - c. the SNCC and La Raza.
   - d. the Nation of Islam and Black Panthers.

8. Charles Reich's book *The Greening of America* was about
    a. huge profits being made my defense contractors during the Vietnam War.
    b. the political power of Irish Americans.
    c. the counterculture generation's attempt to build a new form of community.
    d. the growth of suburbia and planned garden communities.

9. Soldiers who fought in Vietnam were NOT
    a. significantly younger than those who fought in WWII.
    b. less educated than those who fought in WWII.
    c. disproportionately working-class African Americans and Latinos.
    d. welcomed by Vietnamese civilians.

Map Question

10. Most early campus-based protests were in
    a. California and on the East Coast.
    b. Europe and then spread to the United States.
    c. the South and Midwest.
    d. the West and Great Plains.

Short Essay

11. What role did "Sex, drugs, and rock 'n' roll" play in the formation of the counterculture?

Extended Essay

12. Describe the parallel wars that were being fought in Vietnam and in the United States during the Vietnam era.

▶ WARS ON POVERTY ◀

Multiple Choice

13. One of the centerpieces of President Johnson's War on Poverty was the OEO, or Office of _____ Opportunity.
    a. Equal
    b. Economic
    c. Educational
    d. Employment

14. The first major urban riot of 1964–1968 took place in the Watts section of
    a. Newark, New Jersey.
    c. San Francisco, California.
    b. Los Angeles, California.
    d. Detroit, Michigan.

15. The Kerner Commission concluded that the basic cause of the widespread racial violence of the mid-1960s was
    a. criminal lawlessness.
    c. the Vietnam War and unequal rights.
    b. campus radical agitation.
    d. white racism.

16. Which one of the following statements is true?
    a. Spending on social welfare between 1960 and 1974 more than doubled.
    b. Most social welfare payments went to help the poor.
    c. The War on Poverty placed great emphasis on urban problems.
    d. Urban renewal programs were generally beneficial to poor people.

Map Question

17. Which one of the following southern cities did NOT experience an urban uprising between 1965 and 1968?
    a. Atlanta
    c. Birmingham
    b. Memphis
    d. Jackson

Short Essay

18. What led to the urban uprisings of the 1960s?

Extended Essay

19. Evaluate the successes and failures of the War on Poverty.

▶ 1968 ◀

Multiple Choice

20. Which one of the following was NOT a result of the Tet Offensive?
    a. The North Vietnamese lost about one fifth of their total forces.
    b. The Vietcong invaded large cities in South Vietnam.
    c. The United States won a major military victory.
    d. Opposition to the war decreased.

21. Which one of the following has the LEAST in common with the other three?
    a. Richard Daley
    b. Eugene McCarthy
    c. Hubert Humphrey
    d. Lyndon Johnson

Map Question

22. Which one of the following cities was not a site of a major battle of the Tet Offensive?
    a. Saigon
    b. Hue
    c. Hanoi
    d. Danang

Short Essay

23. How did Hubert Humphrey become the Democratic presidential nominee in 1968?

▶ THE POLITICS OF IDENTITY ◀

Multiple Choice

24. Which one of the following is NOT correctly matched to the group it represents?
    a. SDS: Students for a Democratic Society
    b. GLF: Gay Liberation Front
    c. AIM: Asian Independence Movement
    d. NOW: National Organization for Women

25. The galvanizing incident in the Gay Pride movement was
    a. the occupation of Alcatraz prison.
    b. the Stonewall Riot.
    c. a sense of "blowouts" by high school students.
    d. the publication of *Sexual Politics.*

26. Martin Luther King, Jr. is to African Americans as _____ is to Chicano agricultural workers.
    a. Sal Castro   c. David Sanchez
    b. Diego Rivera   d. Cesar Chavez

27. Which one of the following authors is not correctly matched to his or her work?
    a. Stokely Carmichael/*Black Power*
    b. Betty Friedan/*Sexual Politics*
    c. Maxine Hong Kingston/*Woman Warrior*
    d. Vine Deloria, Jr./*Custer Died for Your Sins*

28. Which one of the following is NOT an example of cultural nationalism?
    a. consciousness raising groups
    b. Kwanzaa
    c. Chicanismo
    d. Asian American Studies programs

29. The American Indian Movement was most supported by
    a. Indian tribal leaders.
    b. the Bureau of Indian Affairs.
    c. young urban Indians.
    d. Indians who lived on reservations.

30. U.S. backing of Ferdinand Marcos was protested by
    a. the Black Panthers.
    b. Asian Americans.
    c. Chicanos.
    d. American Indians.

Map Question

31. These two states had an increase in the area added to Indian reservations by 1976:
    a. New Mexico and Arizona.
    c. Kansas and Oklahoma.
    b. Oregon and Nevada.
    d. North and South Dakota.

Short Essay

32. What were the goals of the Black Power movement?

Extended Essay

33. Compare and contrast the women's liberation movement to the Black Power movement.

▶ THE NIXON PRESIDENCY ◀

Multiple Choice

34. The great increase in war protests nationwide culminating in the tragedies at Kent State and Jackson State came about from this policy decision:
    a. Operation Rolling Thunder.
    c. the Tet Offensive.
    b. My Lai search-and-destroy.
    d. the bombing of Cambodia.

35. "Ping-pong diplomacy" symbolized the dramatic changes Nixon made in U.S. policy toward
    a. North Vietnam.
    c. the People's Republic of China.
    b. the Soviet Union.
    d. the Middle East crisis.

36. SALT was a major breakthrough treaty between the United States and the Soviet Union, with the "A" signifying its core of the agreement. The "A" refers to
    a. Air space.
    c. Asian.
    b. Arms.
    d. Atlantic.

Map Question

37. Which one of the following northern states that he had lost in 1960 was won by Nixon in 1968?
    a. New York
    b. Pennsylvania
    c. Michigan
    d. Illinois

Short Essay

38. What led to Nixon's victory in the 1968 presidential election?

Extended Essay

39. What factors led to the U. S. withdrawal from Vietnam?

▶ WATERGATE ◀

Multiple Choice

40. Which one of the following is NOT a regime that Nixon sent arms to during his administration?
    a. Shah of Iran
    b. Botha of South Africa
    c. Marcos of the Philippines
    d. Allende of Chile

41. Which one of the following statements is true?
    a. Nixon was the second president to be impeached.
    b. Nixon was the first president to resign from office.
    c. Nixon was successful in suppressing the Pentagon Papers.
    d. Nixon was not directly involved in the Watergate break-in.

Short Essay

42. What was the role of the media in the Watergate scandal?

Extended Essay

43. Evaluate Nixon's foreign policy successes and failures.

▶ CHRONOLOGY QUESTIONS ◀

Multiple Choice

44. Which one of the following lists the correct chronological order of events?
    (1) The Pentagon papers were published.
    (2) Vietnam Veterans Against the War was formed.
    (3) The Watergate break-in occurred.
    (4) Vietnam peace talks began in Paris.

    a. 2, 4, 1, 3   c. 4, 1, 2, 3
    b. 3, 2, 4, 1   d. 1, 3, 2, 4

45. Which one of the following does NOT happen in 1964?
    a. Johnson declares a war on poverty
    b. Gulf of Tonkin resolution
    c. Watts uprising
    d. free speech movement begins at Berkeley

46. 1969 marks the high tide of the counterculture
    a. at University of California at Berkeley.
    b. in the "Summer of Love."
    c. with the Sheep's Meadow antiwar rally.
    d. at the Woodstock music festival.

ANSWERS-CHAPTER 29

American Communities
  1. a, pp. 903–904

Vietnam: America's Longest War
  2. a, p. 905
  3. c, p. 906
  4. p. 906
  5. p. 907

A Generation in Conflict
  6. b, p.908
  7. a, p. 909
  8. c, p. 909
  9. d, pp. 911–912
  10. a, p. 910
  11. pp. 908–909
  12. pp. 909–912

Wars on Poverty
  13. b, p. 912
  14. b, p. 916
  15. d, p. 916
  16. a, p. 914
  17. c, p. 915
  18. pp. 914–916
  19. pp. 912–914

1968
  20. d, pp. 917–918
  21. b, p. 919
  22. c, p. 917
  23. p. 919

The Politics of Identity
  24. c, p. 921
  25. b, pp. 923–926
  26. d, pp. 924–925
  27. b, pp. 922–923, 927
  28. a, pp. 922–923, 925, 927
  29. c, p. 927
  30. b, p. 928
  31. a, p. 926
  32. pp. 920–922
  33. pp. 920–924

The Nixon Presidency
  34. d, p. 930
  35. c, p. 931
  36. b, p. 931
  37. d, p. 929
  38. pp. 928–929
  39. pp. 905–911, 917–919, 929–931

Watergate
  40. b, p. 932
  41. b, pp. 933, 935
  42. pp. 933, 935
  43. pp. 931–932

Chronology Questions
  44. a, p. 934
  45. c, p. 934
  46. d, p. 934

CHAPTER 30

The Conservative Ascendancy, 1974–1987

SURVEY

Chapter Overview: This chapter covers the economic problems of the Ford and Carter administrations and their inability to solve them. Local political activity increased but did not expand nationally. A new conservatism driven by a revived religious right was energetic but failed to solve the nation's malaise. Americans began to recognize the high cost of the Cold War as President Carter tried to build a foreign policy around moral principles. His mixed success and the Iran hostage crisis paved the way for Ronald Reagan's election, bringing with it a consolidation of the conservative principles that had gained increasing popularity. While the wealthy prospered under Reaganomics, the gap between rich and poor became wider and the country struggled with problems of environmental degradation, drugs, AIDS, and homelessness. Reagan revived a strong anticommunist basis for foreign policy, but the end of his administration saw an improvement of relations with the Soviet Union, which was engaged in internal reforms that eased Cold War tensions.

Before you begin reading, turn to the CHRONOLOGY at the end of the chapter. Review it to orient yourself in space and time and understand who the leading characters are in the story this chapter will tell. Look for cause and effect relationships. Note unfamiliar terms that you will be learning about. Use the tips and questions at the beginning of Chapter 17 of the Study Guide as a guide for your use of the time line. Return to the CHRONOLOGY after you have read the chapter to see how much you have learned.

QUESTIONS/READ

As you read each section, use the questions to help you focus on the major themes. Use them as a way to organize note-taking as you read. The objective is for you to be able to answer these questions after you have read the chapter and completed the study skills exercises. Be on the lookout for important terms that you should be able to identify (see the study skills section in Chapter 18 of the Study Guide for tips on how to fully identify these important terms), and do the map exercises as you go along.

AMERICAN COMMUNITIES:
* Describe how the community of Orange County, California transformed American conservatism and American politics between 1960 and 1980.
* **Identify:** Howard Jarvis, Proposition 13, "born again," Chuck Smith, Calvary Chapel

THE OVEREXTENDED SOCIETY:
* Explain stagflation, the problems that perpetuated it, and federal government response during the administrations of Ford and Carter.
* Describe the energy crisis and its relation to economic problems.

- Outline the issues of the 1976 election, comparing and contrasting Gerald Ford and Jimmy Carter.
- **Identify:** OPEC, energy czar, Department of Energy, outsourcing, Title VII of the Civil Rights Act, National Labor Relations Board rulings, Sunbelt, Snowbelt/Rustbelt, golden age migration, black migration, Monongahela Valley, Clairton, disinvestment, Betty Ford, deregulation
- **Map exercises:** *1970s: Oil Consumption:* (p. 942) What does OPEC mean and what countries are part of it? What happened to the price of oil and energy prices in the 1970s? What happened in the economy? What does stagflation mean? What two unanticipated consequences happened? How did oil production change for various countries during the period?
  Population Shifts, 1970–1980: (p. 943) What overall shifts occurred in the population? What two events coincided to cause this? What states gained 20% or more in population? What states had a loss or only a small gain? In what general area(s) were the states that had a 10–19.9 percent gain? What northern state is in that category?
  Election of 1976: (p. 946) What areas of the country did Carter carry? Which sections did Ford carry?

COMMUNITIES AND POLITICS:
- Summarize the activities of the new urban politics.
- Discuss examples of the endangered environment and the steps that were taken to protect it.
- Describe the trends that characterized small-town America.
- **Identify:** Community Development Act of 1974, COPS, ACORN, Community Development Corporations, Community Boards, National Commission on Neighborhoods, gentrification, Three Mile Island, Love Canal, *Silent Spring,* Frances Moore Lappe, Barry Commoner, Audubon Society, Wilderness Society, Sierra Club, Greenpeace, Environmental Protection Agency, Alaska Pipeline, "exurbia," *Small is Beautiful*

THE NEW CONSERVATISM:
- Describe the new conservatism and the groups that made up the growth of conservative voters.
- **Identify:** New Right, "born again," Jerry Falwell, Moral Majority, Pat Robertson, American Enterprise Institute, Heritage Foundation, Phyllis Schlafly, ERA, *Roe v. Wade,* National Right to Life Committee, Tom Wolfe, "Me Decade," Christopher Lasch's *The Culture of Narcissism,* the human potential movement, Sun Myung Moon, Jim Jones

ADJUSTING TO A NEW WORLD:
- Outline the various foreign policy problems of the Ford and Carter administrations and how they responded to them.
- Analyze how economic and foreign policy problems along with the growth of the New Right led to the Republican victory in the 1980 election.
- **Identify:** "No More Vietnams," Helsinki conference agreement, SALT II, Walter Lippman, human rights, "rogue elephants," Panama Canal treaties, Camp David Accords, Menachem Begin, Anwar el-Sadat, Cyrus Vance, Zbigniew Brzezinski, Anastasio Somoza, Andrew Young, Nigeria and Angola, Afghanistan, Carter Doctrine, Presidential Directive 59, Iran hostage crisis, Ayatollah Ruholla Khomeini, Mohammed Reza Pahlavi, "crisis of confidence" speech

THE REAGAN REVOLUTION:

- Explain the successes and limitations of the Reagan Revolution, especially its contribution to the cycle of recession, recovery, and fiscal crisis.
- Describe the candidates, issues, and outcome of the election of 1984.
- **Identify:** the great communicator, supply-side economics/Reaganomics, George Gilder, Economic Recovery Tax Act of 1981, Omnibus Reconciliation Act of 1981, PATCO, deregulation, James Watt, Drew Lewis, Allen Greenspan, Ivan Boesky, Michael Millken, junk bonds, insider trading, Drexel Burnham Lambert, "Black Moday" of 1987
- **Map exercise:** *The Election of 1980:* (p. 957) What group of voters did Reagan attract? What was the extent of his victory and Carter's loss?

BEST OF TIMES, WORST OF TIMES:

- Describe the factors that contributed to the widening gap between rich and poor in the 1970s and 1980s.
- Discuss the impact of poverty on women and minorities.
- Outline the problems that accompanied the growth of a two-tiered society, including the epidemics of drugs, AIDS, and homelessness.
- **Identify:** Tom Wolfe, "plutography," "yuppies," Allan Bakke, feminization of poverty, AFDC, NWRO, "crack," war on drugs, C. Everett Koop, ACT-UP

REAGAN'S FOREIGN POLICY:

- Trace the policy of President Reagan and the evil empire and how it changed during his administration.
- Explain the Reagan Doctrine and how it applied to Reagan's foreign policy in Central America.
- **Identify:** SDI, Caribbean Basin Initiative, Grenada, El Salvador and Nicaragua, Sandinistas, Somoza, Contras, Boland Amendment, Gorbachev, glasnost, perestroika, Iran-Contra Affai, Beirut, Ayatollah Khomeini, Muammar el-Qaddafi, the National Security Council, William Casey, John Poindexter, Oliver North, Tower Report
- **Map exercises:** *The United States in Central America, 1978–1990:* (p. 967) What happened to U.S. intervention in Central America under Reagan? What areas were the major areas of concentration? Be able to locate the major countries, including island countries and Grenada. Compare this map to those on pages 670 and 857. What countries has the United States been consistently involved in?
  The United States in the Middle East in the 1980s: (p. 969) What were the various areas of U.S. involvement in the 1980s? Be able to identify the countries of the Middle East as well as the following: Sinai Peninsula, West Bank, Gaza Strip, Golan Heights, Beirut, Baghdad, Basra, Teheran, Persian Gulf, Strait of Hormuz, and Suez Canal.

CONCLUSION:

- Explain the new conservative coalition and evaluate its successes and failures.

REVIEW QUESTIONS: Use these to check your grasp of the major chapter themes. It is good practice to write out essay answers to these questions.

STUDY SKILLS EXERCISES

1. Vocabulary:

cartel, p. 941	supply side, p. 958
agribusiness, p. 942	deficit, p. 959
apathy, p. 945	underwriting, p. 960
meltdown, p. 948	disparity, p. 963
evangelical, p. 950	paramilitary, p. 967
cults, p. 952	sordid, p. 968

2. Making connections:

- Compare the decline of the civil rights movement in the 1970s and 1980s to the decline after Reconstruction.
- Compare the South's share of sunbelt success to the idea of the New South. Would Henry Woodfin Grady approve?
- How did many of the foreign policy issues Carter dealt with illustrate the consequences of policies dating from the 1870s?
- Your text states that Vance was the first secretary of state in 65 years to resign over principle. Who was the previous one?
- How well do you think Presidents Carter and Wilson would have coincided on foreign policy principle? Do you find any irony in both of them having secretaries of state resigning?
- It was not uncommon for commentators to compare the United States of the 1980s to the United States of the 1920s. Analyze and evaluate the validity of such a comparison.
- To what extent do you think Reagan's shift from a New Deal Democrat to a Republican parallels a shift of a significant number of American voters?
- Compare the new poverty of the 1970s and 1980s to the poverty issues discussed in the Great Society.

3. Reflections:

- How would you have voted (or how did you vote) and why in the 1976, 1980, and 1984 elections?
- Should Carter have paid more attention to Cyrus Vance's or Zbigniew Brzezinski's advice in foreign policy?
- How significant is grass-roots politics to you as a way to solve problems?
- Was the "me decade" new or was the United States returning to an earlier era after a period of high involvement and expectation? Do you agree with Tom Wolfe or Christopher Lasch in the first place? Why or why not?
- Consider whether war is an appropriate metaphor for dealing with problems like drugs or diseases.

RECITE/REVIEW

REVIEW QUESTIONS: This section has a sampling of multiple choice, short essay, and extended essay questions that you should be able to answer when you have completed the chapter and used other study techniques. To help you in reviewing the material, questions have been grouped according to the major sections of the chapter. Of course, you cannot expect your tests to be set up in this way.

▶ AMERICAN COMMUNITIES ◀

Multiple Choice

1. If you were a conservative voter in Orange County, you would be LEAST likely to support
   - a. big government.
   - b. tax cuts.
   - c. the Vietnam War.
   - d. law and order.

▶ THE OVEREXTENDED SOCIETY ◀

Multiple Choice

2. Which one of the following is NOT an example of the economic problems of the United States in the early to mid-1970s?
   - a. U.S. unemployment reached 9 percent by 1975.
   - b. U.S. imported one third of its crude oil.
   - c. U.S. steel companies invested in overseas mining companies.
   - d. U.S. southern cities continued to lose African American population.

3. Critics called Carter a Democrat who talked and thought like a Republican. Which one of the following was NOT one of his actions that seemed to reinforce that?
   - a. He sought to reduce the scale of federal government.
   - b. He deregulated airlines and banks from federal control.
   - c. He defended existing entitlement programs.
   - d. He opposed comprehensive health coverage.

4. The Sunbelt states were LEAST likely to spend their tax dollars on
   - a. education.
   - b. roads.
   - c. police forces.
   - d. sanitation systems.

Map Questions

5. Which one of the following had the MOST growth in oil production between 1973 and 1984?
   - a. OPEC producers
   - b. Soviet Union
   - c. United States
   - d. Mexico

6. The only northern state to experience a high gain of population in the 1970s was
   - a. Vermont.
   - b. New York.
   - c. New Hampshire.
   - d. Iowa.

7. Which one of the following southern states did NOT vote for Carter in the 1976 election?
   - a. Florida
   - b. Texas
   - c. Virginia
   - d. Kentucky

Short Essay

8. What factors contributed to the economic problems of the 1970s?

▶ COMMUNITIES AND POLITICS ◀

Multiple Choice

9. All of the following cities elected black mayors in the 1970s EXCEPT
   a. Atlanta, Georgia.
   b. Gary, Indiana.
   c. Madison, Wisconsin.
   d. Detroit, Michigan.

10. Three Mile Island showed the problems associated with
    a. toxic waste dumping.
    b. the use of DDT.
    c. damming wetlands for housing development.
    d. the use of nuclear power.

11. Frances Moore Lappe and Barry Commoner both argued that people had to accept the
    a. relationship of consumption and the environment.
    b. restoration of "traditional family values."
    c. balance and limits of "small is beautiful."
    d. fact that the United States could not run and police the whole world.

Short Essay

12. How did city dwellers respond to urban problems in the 1970s?

▶ THE NEW CONSERVATISM ◀

Multiple Choice

13. Which one of the following was NOT an example of the new conservatism?
    a. passage of Proposition 13 in California
    b. decrease in voter participation among conservatives
    c. popularity of the Moral Majority
    d. Phyllis Schafly's STOP ERA

14. The first major politician to realize the power of the New Right and appeal directly to it for fundraising was
    a. Ronald Reagan.
    b. Jerry Ford.
    c. Jesse Helms.
    d. George Bush.

15. In terms of conservatism, which one of the following has the LEAST in common with the other three?
    a. Sun Myung Moon
    b. Jim Jones
    c. Pat Robertson
    d. Jerry Falwell

Extended Essay

16. Analyze the emergence of American conservatism in the late 1970s.

▶ Adjusting to a New World ◀

Multiple Choice

17. The 1975 conference in Helsinki, Finland moved away from the Cold War days by
    a. establishing a second SALT treaty.
    b. accepting the boundaries of countries drawn after World War II.
    c. having all major powers agree to stay neutral in the Arab-Israeli conflict.
    d. limiting world arms sales.

18. Which one of the following areas came out successfully for Carter in terms of his policies?
    a. Iran
    b. Panama
    c. Nicaragua
    d. El Salvador

19. Which one of the following was NOT a part of the Camp David Accords?
    a. Egypt recognized the existence of Israel as a state.
    b. Israel gave the Sinai Peninsula back to Egypt.
    c. Egypt agreed to supply oil to the United States.
    d. The "legitimate rights of the Palestinians" were vaguely agreed to.

20. Soviet invasion of Afghanistan prompted critics to call it the "Russian Vietnam" because of this similarity:
    a. they were caught in an unwinnable civil war with guerrillas against them.
    b. they fabricated a pretext for moving in there in the first place.
    c. they were trying to counter U.S. influence in Afghanistan.
    d. major protests broke out in the Soviet Union.

21. Which one of the following caused Secretary of State Cyrus Vance to resign?
    a. Carter's attempt at military rescue of the American hostages in Iran
    b. the Carter Doctrine
    c. Carter's backing of a repressive government in El Salvador
    d. Carter's firing of UN ambassador Andrew Young

Extended Essay

22. Analyze Jimmy Carter's foreign policy strengths and weaknesses.

▶ REAGAN REVOLUTION ◀

Multiple Choice

23. Reagan's experience in being a national spokesman for this company helped him become a significant public figure and perfect his style and conservative message:
    a. General Motors.
    b. Westinghouse.
    c. General Electric.
    d. Chrysler.

24. Which one of the following was NOT an element of Reagan's speeches?
    a. celebrating corporate America
    c. opposition to radical trade unions
    b. dangers of big government
    d. support for New Deal liberalism

25. Which one of the following is characteristic of supply-side economics?
    a. increase in defense spending
    c. increase in social welfare spending
    b. increase in the capital gains tax
    d. increase in the maximum income tax rate

26. The Omnibus Reconciliation Act of 1981
    a. cut over 200 social and cultural programs.
    b. was also called Gramm-Rudman and aimed at controlling the deficit.
    c. cut income and corporate taxes.
    d. deregulated numerous government agency rulings.

27. Which one of the following was NOT something that had already been increased by President Carter and continued by President Reagan?
    a. defense spending
    b. human resource spending
    c. revival of Cold War
    d. deregulation

Map Question

28. In the 1980 election, Republican candidate Reagan carried
    a. the Far West.
    b. the South.
    c. New England.
    d. all states but six.

Short Essay

29. What were Reagan's vulnerable issues in the 1984 election and why wasn't Mondale able to defeat him?

Extended Essay

30. Evaluate the success or failure of Reagan's economic policies over his two terms in office.

▶ BEST OF TIMES, WORST OF TIMES ◀

Multiple Choice

31. If you liked to live vicariously through what Tom Wolfe called "plutography," then you liked watching
   a. commercials.
   b. Disney cartoons.
   c. *Lifestyles of the Rich and Famous.*
   d. spectacular special effects and science fiction with traditional values.

32. Which one of the following did Americans consider the nation's number one problem in the 1980s?
   a. AIDS
   b. widespread drug use
   c. homelessness
   d. teenage pregnancy

Short Essay

33. How was the two-tiered society defined by race?

Extended Essay

34. Use specific examples to show why the 1980s were the best of times and the worst of times.

▶ REAGAN'S FOREIGN POLICY ◀

Multiple Choice

35. Congress tried to control the problem of covert war in Nicaragua by passing the amendment known as
    - a. Gramm-Rudman.
    - b. Tower.
    - c. Boland.
    - d. Iran-Contra.

36. President Reagan's CBI meant
    - a. Communist Barrier International.
    - b. Cut Back Immigration.
    - c. Compunications Belt Initiative.
    - d. Caribbean Basin Initiative.

37. Which one of the following was NOT a Latin American area to which President Reagan sent military aid, advisors, or troops?
    - a. El Salvador
    - b. Nicaragua
    - c. Grenada
    - d. Cuba

Map Questions

38. Which one of the following countries was NOT involved in the fight with the Sandinista rebels?
    - a. Honduras
    - b. El Salvador
    - c. Guatemala
    - d. Nicaragua

39. The Iran-Iraq War began in 1980 with an attack on
    - a. Basra.
    - b. Tehran.
    - c. Beirut.
    - d. Kuwait.

Short Essay

40. How did Gorbachev attempt to improve the Soviet Union's economic performance?

41. What were the major issues involved in the Iran-Contra Scandal?

Extended Essay

42. Why did the Reagan Administration believe U.S. interests were so greatly involved in Central America?

▶ CHRONOLOGY QUESTIONS ◀

Multiple Choice

43. Which one of the following did NOT occur in 1978?
    a. *Bakke* v. *University of California* decision
    b. California passes Proposition 13
    c. Middle East peace accord at Camp David
    d. Three Mile Island nuclear accident

44. The *Roe* v. *Wade* decision legalized abortion in
    a. 1973.   c. 1982.
    b. 1977.   d. 1985.

45. Which one of the following lists the correct chronological order of events?
    (1) Arab embargo sparks oil crisis
    (2) Iran–Contra hearings
    (3) Marines killed in Beirut terrorist bombing
    (4) American hostages seized in Iran

    a. 3, 1, 4, 2   c. 1, 4, 3, 2
    b. 4, 1, 2, 3   d. 1, 3, 2, 4

46. Unemployment at 9 percent occurred in 1975. Inflation at 13.5 percent occurred in
    a. 1975.   c. 1980.
    b. 1978.   d. 1982.

ANSWERS-CHAPTER 30

American Communities
   1. a, p. 940

The Overextended Society
   2. d, pp. 941, 944–945
   3. c, p. 945
   4. a, p. 944
   5. b, p. 942
   6. c, p. 943
   7. c, p. 94
   8. pp. 941–942

Communities and Politics
   9. c, p. 946
   10. d, p. 948
   11. a, p. 949
   12. pp. 947–948

The New Conservatism
   13. b, pp. 950–951
   14. c, p. 950
   15. b, pp. 950, 952
   16. pp. 950–952

Adjusting to a New World
   17. b, p. 953
   18. b, pp. 955–956
   19. c, pp. 954–955
   20. a, p. 955
   21. a, pp. 955–956
   22. pp. 953–956

Reagan Revolution
   23. c, p. 958
   24. d, p. 958
   25. a, p. 959
   26. a, p. 959
   27. b, pp. 954, 955, 959
   28. d, p. 957
   29. pp. 959–960
   30. pp. 959–961

Best of Times, Worst of Times
   31. c, p. 962
   32. b, p. 964
   33. p. 963
   34. pp. 961–965

Regan's Foreign Policy
   35. c, p. 966
   36. d, p. 966
   37. d, p. 966
   38. c, p. 967
   39. a, p. 969
   40. pp. 967–968
   41. pp. 968–969
   42. pp. 966–967

Chronology Questions
   43. d, p. 970
   44. a, p. 970
   45. c, p. 970
   46. c, p. 970

CHAPTER 31

Toward A Transnational America, Since 1988

SURVEY

Chapter Overview: This chapter covers the new world order that marks the state of affairs at the beginning of the twentyfirst century. The collapse of communism and the end of the Cold War changed the nature of America's foreign policy commitments. The 1990s saw a return of the Democrats to the presidency and a booming economy based largely in the new high-tech and service industries that created an electronic culture. New immigrants from Latin America and Asia are changing the face of American society and culture. Despite the end of the Cold War, Americans experienced anxiety fueled by racial and cultural tensions as well as terrorism at home and abroad. There was a resurgence of the right in the middle of the 1990s that led to an impeachment process based largely on partisan concerns and the personal life of President Clinton. Despite the booming economy, Al Gore was unable to keep the White House for the Democrats in a controversial election in 2000. President Bush faced international issues such as global warming and global trade as well as increased international terrorism that manifested in the attacks on the World Trade Center and the Pentagon in 2001. President Bush declared a long-term, world-wide war on terrorism.

Before you begin reading, turn to the CHRONOLOGY at the end of the chapter. Review it to orient yourself in space and time and understand who the leading characters are in the story this chapter will tell. Look for cause and effect relationships. Note unfamiliar terms that you will be learning about. Use the tips and questions at the beginning of Chapter 17 of the Study Guide as a guide for your use of the time line. Return to the CHRONOLOGY after you have read the chapter to see how much you have learned.

QUESTIONS/READ

As you read each section, use the questions to help you focus on the major themes. Use them as a way to organize note-taking as you read. The objective is for you to be able to answer these questions after you have read the chapter and completed the study skills exercises. Be on the lookout for important terms that you should be able to identify (see the study skills section in Chapter 18 of the Study Guide for tips on how to fully identify these important terms), and do the map exercises as you go along.

AMERICAN COMMUNITIES:
- Describe how the World Trade Center could have been called a transnational community.

A NEW WORLD ORDER:
- Explain how the end of the Cold War changed America's foreign policy.
- Describe America's military involvement in the Middle East and the Balkans.
- Describe the role of human rights concerns in directing American foreign policy.

- **Identify:** Gorbachev, the Berlin Wall, Commonwealth of Independent States, Operation Desert Shield, Operation Desert Storm, Saddam Hussein, Kuwait, "Nintendo war," DN shells, sanctions, Declaration of Principles in Oslo, Itzakh Rabin, Yassar Arafat, Israeli "settlements," Saudi Arabia, Osama bin Laden, Al-Qaeda, William Christopher, Madeline Albright, Bosnia, "ethnic cleansing," Serbs, Croats, Muslims, Slobodan Milosevic, Dayton Accords, Kosovo, ethnic Albanians, International War Crimes Tribunal, Universal Declaration of Human Rights, NGOs, Human Rights Watch, Tiannamen Square, Most Favored Nation

CHANGING AMERICAN COMMUNITIES:
- Summarize the dramatic socio-economic changes in America, including a shift to a service-based and high-tech information economy and a more electronic culture.
- Discuss the issues of the 1992 presidential campaign as they relate to the above trends.
- Explain the successes and limitations of the Reagan Revolution through the senior Bush and Clinton administrations.
- Describe how new immigrants are changing the face of American society.
- **Identify:** Gramm-Rudman Act, Perot, political gridlock, Welfare Reform Act, Alan Greenspan, NAFTA, GATT, WTO, *maquiladora,* NASDAQ, "downsizing," venture capital, "dot.com," Silicon Valley, consumer electronics, Pacific Rim, "global village," "narrowcasting," MTV, cyberspace, ARPANET, "hackers," Internet, World Wide Web, "information highway," "day trading," "home pages," Rupert Murdoch, Immigration Act of 1965, The Immigration Reform and Control Act of 1986, "Spanish Harlem," "World Beat" music, "chain migration"
- **Map and Chart exercises:** *The Election of 1992* (p. 982) What states/regions were carried by each candidate? How much of the popular vote did Ross Perot get?
  The Internet in the United States (p. 986) What part of the country was reached by the Internet? How would you describe the nature of the network?
  Chart: *Continent of Birth for Immigrants, 1990–2000:* (p. 987) Where did most immigrants to the United States come from in the 1990s? the least?

A NEW AGE OF ANXIETY:
- Outline the conditions that contributed to and reflected racial and cultural divisions in the country.
- Describe the sources of fear that created anxiety in America.
- Describe the goals of Clinton's first term and the resurgence of the right under Gingrich.
- Compare and contrast the issues and outcomes of the 1994 and 1996 elections.
- **Identify:** Rodney King, O. J. Simpson, "racial profiling," War on Drugs, Pan Am flight to Lockerbie Scotland, Antiterrorism and Effective Death Penalty Act, Alfred P. Murrah Federal Building, "Branch Davidians," ATF, David Koresh, Waco, Timothy McVeigh, "Date of Doom," Operation Rescue, Columbine High School, Rush Limbaugh, "Doctor" Laura, multiculturalism, Allan Bloom's *Closing of the American Mind,* Proposition 187, Hillary Rodham Clinton, Defense of Marriage Act, Colorado for Family Values, embryonic stem cell research, Creation Science Movement, Christian Coalition, Newt Gingrich, Contract with America, Whitewater, Kenneth Starr, Paula Jones, Monica Lewinski

THE NEW MILLENNIUM:
- Outline the factors that brought basic assumptions about American life into question at the beginning of the twentyfirst century.

- Describe the candidates, issues, and outcome of the election of 2000.
- Trace the development of globalization and evaluate its effects on developed and developing countries.
- **Identify:** James Jeffords, H. R. Clinton, "Rutherfraud" B. Hayes, global warming, greenhouse gases, Montreal Protocol, Kyoto Protocol, new "colonialism," multinational corporations, the Triad, Wal-Mart Stores, Inc., World Trade Organization, IMF/World Bank, Seattle and Genoa, World Trade Center, Pentagon, Colin Powell, Homeland Security, Osama bin Laden, Al-Qaeda, Taliban
- **Map exercise:** *The Election of 2000* (p. 997) What areas of the country did each candidate carry? Who won the popular vote? Who won the Electoral College? How was the election decided?

CONCLUSION

- Describe how the war on terrorism replaced the Cold War as the focus of American foreign policy.

REVIEW QUESTIONS: Use these to check your grasp of the major chapter themes. It is good practice to write out essay answers to these questions.

STUDY SKILLS EXERCISES

1. Vocabulary:

proliferation, p. 977	fusion, p. 989
federated, p. 980	*in vitro* fertilization, p. 994
détente, p. 981	polemicist, p. 995
entrepreneurship, p. 985	pundits, p. 996
retrenchment, p. 985	bilateralism, p. 997
cyberspace, p. 986	communique, p. 1001
amnesty, p. 988	

2. Making connections:

- Compare and contrast the impeachment processes of Andrew Johnson and Bill Clinton.
- Compare the stock market booms and their aftermaths of the 1920s, 1980s, and 1990s.
- How does the Creation Science Movement connect with the Scopes trial of the 1920s? What are the social conditions that caused the issue of evolution versus creationism to emerge in each time period?
- How does the fear of terrorism resemble the fear of communism at the beginning of the Cold War? What are the similarities and differences in the country's responses? Are there lessons to be learned from the earlier experience?
- President Eisenhower warned Americans about the problems of a military-industrial complex. To what extent do you think this warning continued to be valid?
- How does the racial situation in the year 2000 reflect on the achievements of the civil rights movement?
- Compare the role of the press and freedom of reporters on the battlefield in Vietnam and the Persian Gulf War.
- Carter's critics said he often talked like a Democrat and thought like a Republican. To what extent did Clinton do this while campaigning?
- Compare Carter and Clinton on the relationship between human rights and foreign policy.

3. Reflections:

- How would you have voted (or did you vote) in the, 1992, 1994, 1996, and 2000 elections? What would have been the significant issues to you? If you were registered to vote and didn't, why not?

- Gorbachev said he was going to do something terrible to us—deprive us of an enemy. Who has become the enemy? Is it necessary to see things in that way? How does it affect unity on the one hand and create disunity on the other?

- How do you feel about the ethical dilemma involved in economic sanctions against Iraq?

- Given the controversy surrounding the 2000 presidential election, do you think there should be reforms in the Electoral College system or should it remain as it is? Defend your answer.

RECITE/REVIEW

REVIEW QUESTIONS: This section has a sampling of multiple choice, short essay, and extended essay questions that you should be able to answer when you have completed the chapter and used other study techniques. To help you in reviewing the material, questions have been grouped according to the major sections of the chapter. Of course, you cannot expect your tests to be set up in this way.

▶ AMERICAN COMMUNITIES ◀

Multiple Choice

1. Which one of the following statements is NOT true?
    a. More than 50,000 people worked at the World Trade Center.
    b. The majority of Hispanic New Yorkers in 2001 were Puerto Ricans and Cubans.
    c. Many international companies had offices in the World Trade Center.
    d. Citizens of 81 nations perished in the terrorist attacks of September 11, 2001.

▶ A NEW WORLD ORDER ◀

Multiple Choice

2. Which one of the following is the RESULT of the other three?
    a. reduced standard of living in the Soviet Union
    b. fifteen republics withdraw from the Soviet Union
    c. Communist Party leaders defeated in open elections
    d. Soviets fail in their war in Afghanistan

3. The Persian Gulf War developed when Iraq invaded
    a. Iran.
    b. Kuwait.
    c. Saudi Arabia.
    d. Israel.

4. During the Persian Gulf War, these individuals were accompanied by "military escorts":
    a. United Nations Officials.
    b. Bedouins.
    c. oil well personnel.
    d. reporters.

5. Which one of the following was focused on establishing peace between Israelis and Palestinians during Clinton's first term?
   a. Declaration of Principles in Oslo
   b. Dayton Accords
   c. Most Favored Nation status
   d. Universal Declaration of Human Rights

6. Which one of the following has the LEAST in common with the other three?
   a. Albania
   b. Bosnia
   c. Kosovo
   d. Macedonia

7. Tianamen Square was the site of
   a. Israeli settlements.
   b. NATO bombing.
   c. an attack on prodemocracy demonstrators.
   d. ethnic cleansing.

Short Essay

8. Describe the major events in the collapse of communism during the late 1980s.

9. What were the components of the liberal internationalism that was the core of President Clinton's foreign policy?

Extended Essay

10. What were the long-term effects of the Gulf War in Iraq and throughout the Middle East?

39。

Multiple Choice

11. The goal of the Gramm-Rudman Act was
    a. to bailout the savings and loan industry.
    b. a balanced federal budget.
    c. ending welfare.
    d. promoting free trade.

12. Which one of the following is NOT an example of Clinton's ability to adopt conservative themes?
    a. welfare reform
    b. encouragement of "free trade"
    c. increased federal government control of business
    d. controlled interest rates to check inflation

13. Which one of the following led to the creation of the World Bank?
    a. AFDC
    b. NAFTA
    c. NASDAQ
    d. GATT

14. Which one of the following is the RESULT of the other three?
    a. microelectronics dominates the economy
    b. defense industry spending increases
    c. invention of the semiconductor chip
    d. consumer electronics revolution

15. Which one of the following statements is NOT true?
    a. Television drives the strategies of American politicians.
    b. More than three fourths of American public school classrooms are online.
    c. There are more television sets in the United States than in any other country.
    d. The United States produces 40 percent of the world's television programming.

16. Which one of the following statements is true?
    a. Hispanics settle only in the Southwest and California.
    b. In the 2000 Census, Hispanics were the largest minority group under eighteen years of age.
    c. Japanese immigration is driving the growth in Asian immigrants.
    d. Asians constitute both the largest number and fastest rate of growth among immigrants.

17. Which one of the following does NOT characterize Asian immigrants?
    a. making education a priority
    b. pooling resources to establish small businesses
    c. unskilled Chinese immigrants
    d. "chain migration"

Map Questions

18. Which one of the following areas was the LEAST strong for Clinton in the 1992 election?
    a. Northeast
    b. Midwest
    c. Great Plains
    d. California and Pacific Northwest

19. Which one of the following statements BEST characterizes the presence of the Internet in the United States?
    a. it is confined to the East and West Coasts
    b. it is spread throughout the country
    c. it is available only in large cities
    d. it does not reach Alaska and Hawaii

20. Place of birth for the largest percentage of immigrants in the 1990s was
    a. Europe.
    b. Latin America.
    c. Asia.
    d. Africa.

Short Essay

21. What is NAFTA and what are its results?

22. How has television become more powerful in American culture?

23. How did the Immigration and Reform Act of 1986 relate to the Immigration Act of 1965?

Extended Essay

24. Analyze President Bush's drop in popularity from the end of the Gulf War until the 1992 election.

Multiple Choice

25. The 1992 Los Angeles riot was ignited over the issue of
    a. racial profiling.
    b. tension between African Americans and Latinos.
    c. police brutality.
    d. segregated schools.

26. Which one of the following has the LEAST in common with the others?
    a. Columbine High School
    b. Operation Rescue
    c. Murrah Federal Building
    d. World Trade Center

27. Proposition 187 was concerned with
    a. multiculturalism in schools.
    b. social services for illegal immigrants.
    c. same-sex marriages.
    d. embryonic stem cell research.

28. Which one of the following issues contributed MOST to the Republicans' victory in the 1994 election?
    a. welfare reform
    b. affirmative action
    c. health-care reform
    d. balanced federal budget

29. The Contract with America was
    a. a package of conservative proposals authored by Newt Gingrich.
    b. Hillary Rodham Clinton's proposal for health-care reform.
    c. Robert Dole's campaign platform in the 1996 election.
    d. a conservative response to multiculturalism.

Short Essay

30. Describe the conditions that were contributing to the racial divide in America in the 1990s.

31. What was multiculturalism and what was the conservative response to it?

Extended Essay

32. How did extremism support acts of terrorism both at home and abroad in the 1990s?

▶ THE NEW MILLENNIUM ◀

Multiple Choice

33. Which one of the following statements is NOT true?
    a. American society has become more stratified along the lines of race and class.
    b. New media technologies have made American cultural life more diverse.
    c. The enemies that have replaced the Soviet Union are more fanatic and less predictable.
    d. The New Economy is service-oriented and high tech.

34. Which one of the following does NOT accurately describes the presidential election of 2000?
    a. The winner of the popular vote did not win the Electoral College vote.
    b. The Democrats had the first Jewish candidate for vice-president.
    c. There were no third-party candidates of any significance.
    d. It was the first presidential election to be decided by a vote of the U.S. Supreme Court.

35. Which one of the following has the LEAST in common with the other three?
    a. greenhouse gases   c. Montreal Protocol
    b. development of national forests   d. Kyoto Protocol

36. The Triad is made up of
    a. the UN, the WTO, and the IMF.
    b. the United States, Canada, and Mexico.
    c. North America, Europe, and Japan.
    d. NAFTA, GATT, and the World Bank.

37. The MOST distinctive characteristic of international trade at the end of the twentieth century was
    a. the rate of growth.
    b. the existence of well-organized transnational economies.
    c. the volume of revenue of multinational corporations.
    d. the presence of high tariffs.

38. In the wake of the September 11, 2001, attacks on the World Trade Center and the Pentagon, all of the following occurred EXCEPT
    a. the United States bombed Afghanistan.
    b. Osama bin Laden was tried in the International War Crimes Tribunal.
    c. President Bush created a new Homeland Security agency.
    d. the Department of Justice began investigating suspected terrorists.

Map Question

39. Which one of the following generalizations about the 2000 presidential election is true?
    a. George Bush won the popular vote and the Electoral College.
    b. Al Gore carried all of New England.
    c. The South is solidly Democratic.
    d. Al Gore carried far fewer states than Bush but won the popular vote.

Short Essay

40. What was the Kyoto Protocol and what was the position of the United States on it?

41. What is meant by a new colonialism since World War II?

Extended Essay

42. Outline the pros and cons of the trend toward globalization.

▶ CHRONOLOGY QUESTIONS ◀

Multiple Choice

43. MTV and CNN began broadcasting as cable channels in
    a. 1980.
    b. 1981.
    c. 1987.
    d. 1988.

44. Which one of the following did not happen in 1994?
    a. Republicans win control of the Senate and House
    b. Congress approves GATT
    c. the European Union endorses Kyoto Protocol
    d. California voters approve Proposition 187

45. Which one of the following lists the correct chronological order of events?
    (1) Congress passes Welfare Reform Act
    (2) Rodney King verdict and Los Angeles rioting
    (3) Immigration Reform and Control Act
    (4) Clinton proposes health-care reform

    a. 3, 2, 1, 4   c. 2, 4, 3, 1
    b. 3, 2, 4, 1   d. 4, 3, 1, 2

46. Which one of the following years did not have an incident of international terrorism involving the United States?
    a. 1988
    b. 1993
    c. 1995
    d. 1998

ANSWERS-CHAPTER 31

American Communities
  1. b, pp. 975–976

New World Order
  2. b, pp. 977–978
  3. b, p. 978
  4. d, p. 979
  5. a, p. 980
  6. b, p. 980
  7. c, p. 981
  8. pp. 977–978
  9. p. 981
  10. pp. 979–980

Changing American Communities
  11. b, p. 982
  12. c, pp. 982–983
  13. d, p. 984
  14. a, p. 985
  15. c, p. 987
  16. b, pp. 988–989
  17. c, p. 989
  18. c, p. 982
  19. b, p. 986
  20. b, p. 987
  21. p. 984
  22. pp. 985–986
  23. pp. 987–988
  24. pp. 979, 982

A New Age of Anxiety
  25. c, p. 990
  26. d, pp. 991–992
  27. b, pp. 993–994
  28. c, p. 995
  29. a, p. 995
  30. pp. 990–991
  31. p. 993
  32. pp. 991–992

The New Millennium
  33. b, p. 997
  34. c, pp. 997–998
  35. b, p. 999
  36. c, p. 1000
  37. c, p. 1000
  38. b, pp. 1001–1003
  39. d, p. 997

  40. p. 999
  41. pp. 999–1000
  42. p. 1000

Chronology Questions
  43. b, p. 1002
  44. c, p. 1002
  45. b, p. 1002
  46. c, p. 1002

Maps

CHAPTER 20

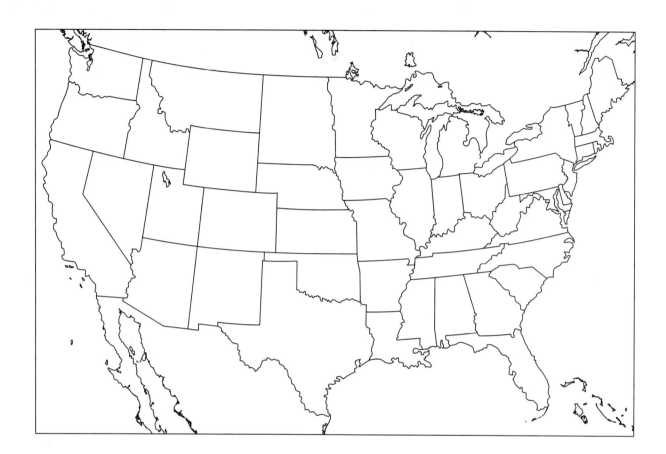

CHAPTER 20

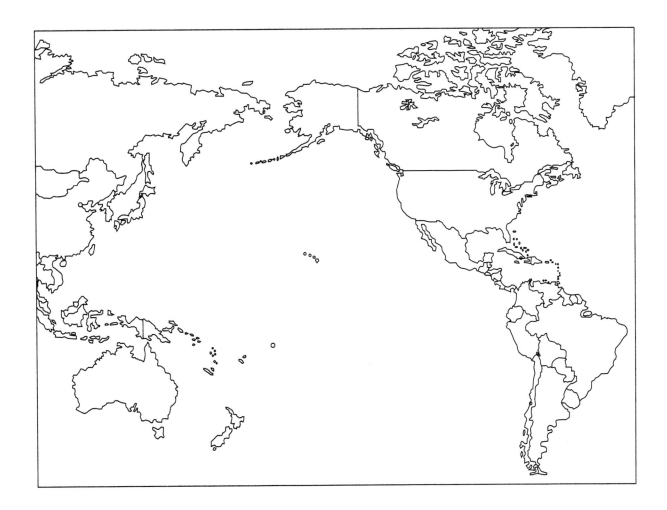

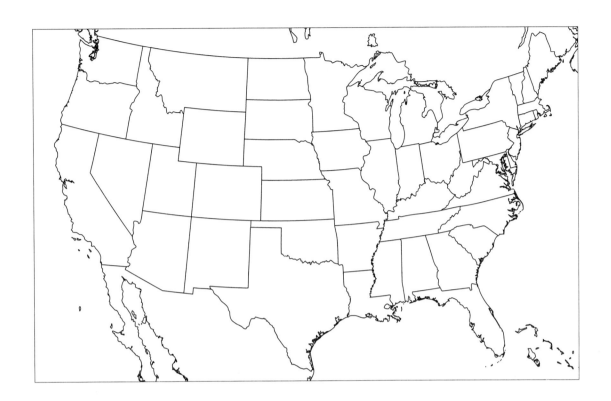

Maps

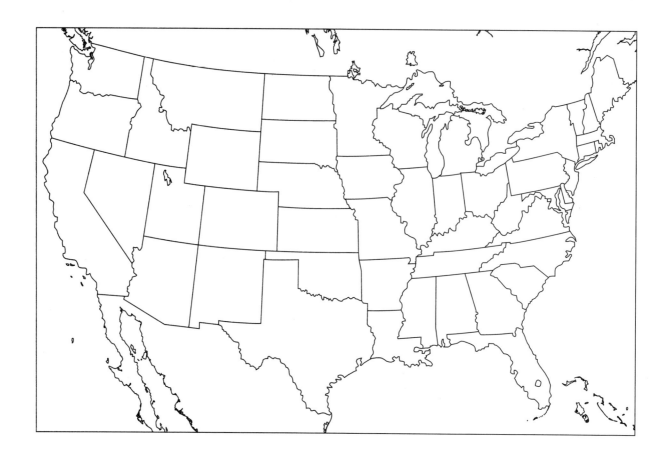

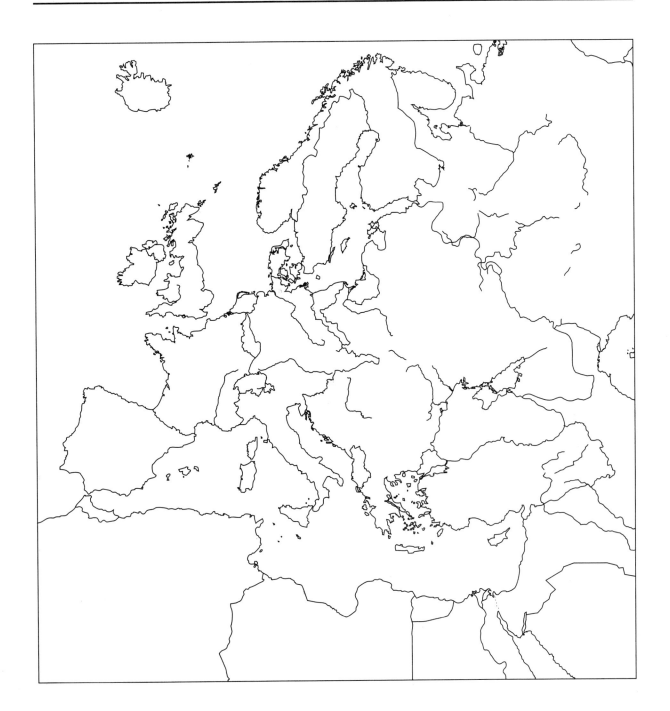

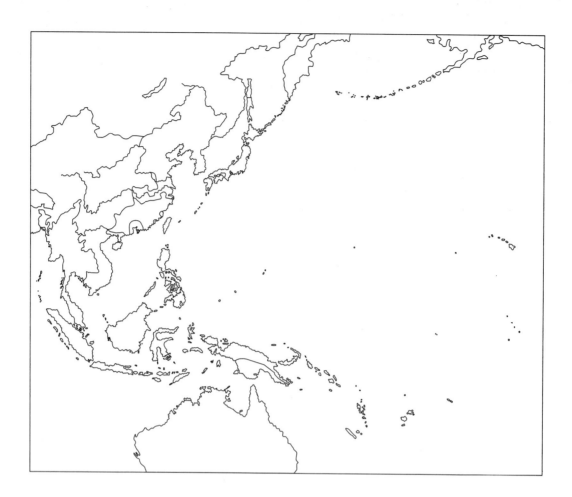

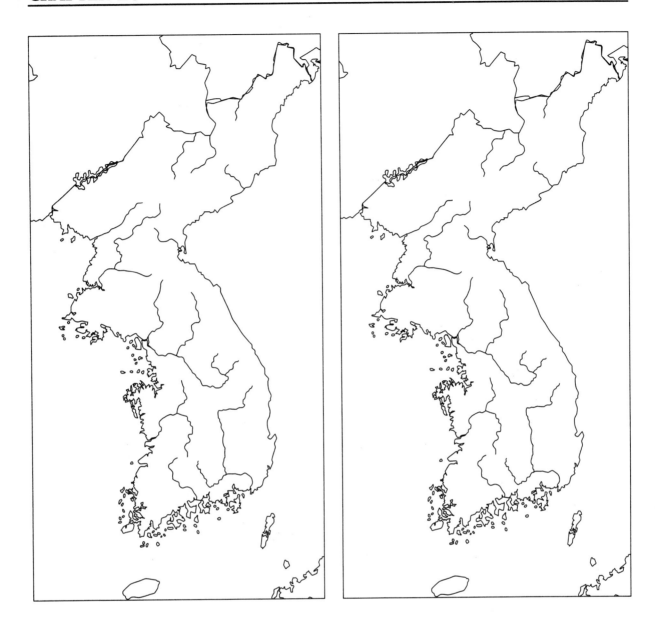

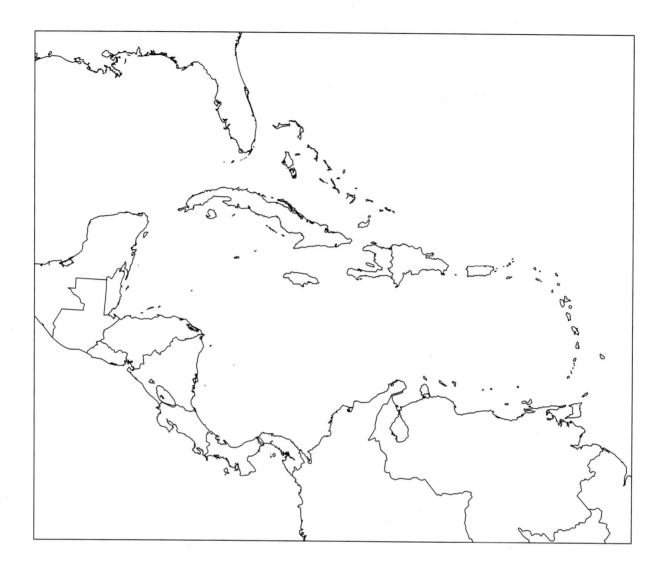

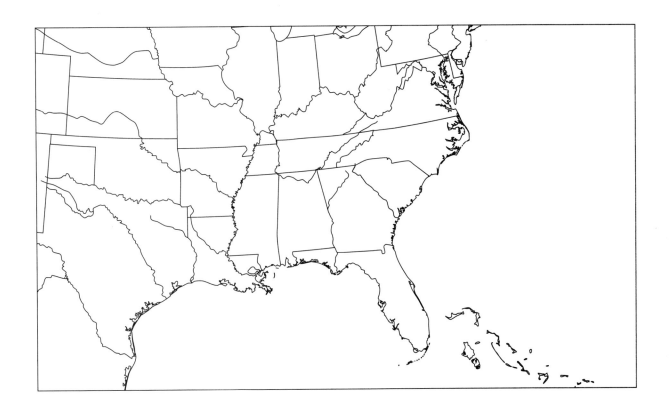

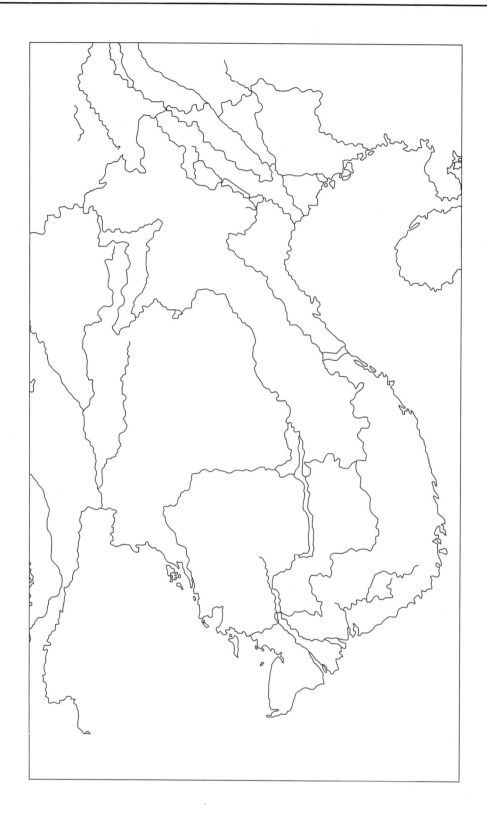

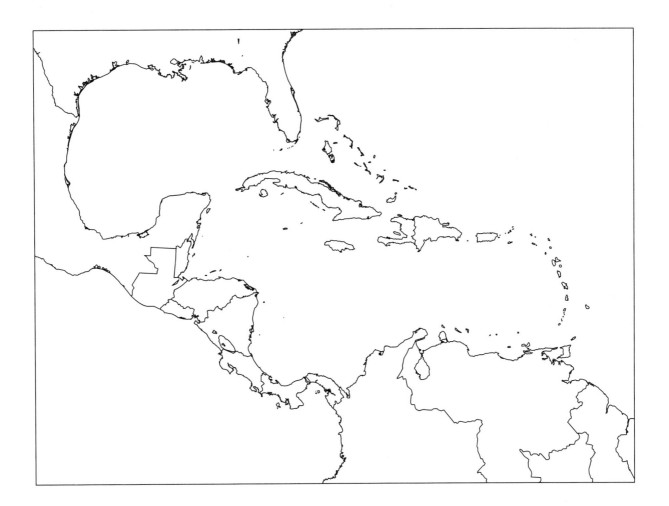

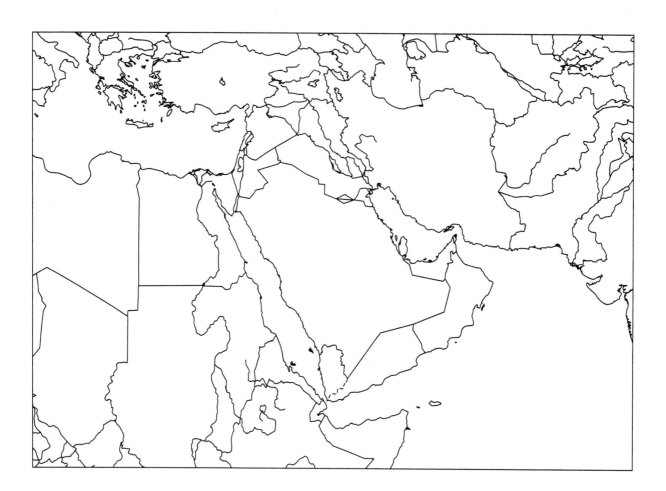